Hole-in-One Nutrition

ROBERT YANG, M.S., C.N., C.S.C.S.
WITH SEAN HYSON, C.S.C.S., C.P.P.S.

Copyright © 2018 Robert Yang. All rights reserved.

No part of this publication may be reproduced or distributed in any form or bay any means, electronic or mechanical, or stored in a database or retrieval system, without prior written permission from the author

ISBN 978-1-7327555-0-5

The information included in this book is for educational purposes only. It is not intended or implied to be a substitute for professional medical advice. The reader should always consult his or her a health-care provider to determine the appropriateness of the information for his or her situation. The advice and strategies contained herein may not be suitable for your situation. This book is sold with the understanding that the author is not engaged in rendering medical, legal, accounting, or other professional services. You should consult with a professional where appropriate. The author shall not be liable for any loss of profit or any other commercial damages, including but not limited to special, incidental, consequential, or other damages.

Hole-in-One Nutrition

A GUIDE TO FUELING BETTER GOLF

ROBERT YANG, M.S., C.N., C.S.C.S.
WITH SEAN HYSON, C.S.C.S., C.P.P.S.

ACKNOWLEDGEMENTS

This book is dedicated to my parents who never told me to work hard and sacrifice. They lived it. Writing this book is a culmination of a lot of hard work and sacrifice that I would not have been able accomplish without them. I also dedicate this book to my wife, Angie. Your love and support is everything. Finally, I dedicate this book to the players and athletes who have taught me more than I have taught them.

CONTENTS

INTRODUCTION

"You can't go into a shop and buy a good game of golf."

—Sam Snead

There's only one thing you want when it comes to your game: to lower your handicap. Like any golfer, you'll try anything. Tweak your swing. Buy the latest and greatest driver or pay a pro for lessons. But the one thing I bet you've never tried is the simplest performance-enhancer of all. It doesn't require spending lots of money or dedicating extra time on the driving range or putting green.

You haven't tried nutrition.

If you've experimented with every driver out there, watched every instructional video, hired experts to reengineer your swing for maximum trajectory, yet you still can't break 80, the problem probably isn't with your golf game. It's how you're fueling it.

If you've followed pro golf over the past two decades, you've seen many of its top players embrace fitness, the kind of workouts common with people who compete in more physically rigorous sports: football players, fighters, and bodybuilders.

Tiger Woods has been open about his use of weight training to transform his once lanky body into a much more powerful and athletic physique. It's helped make him one of the longest drivers in the history of the sport and arguably one of the best players that's ever played. Since the introduction of strength and conditioning to pro golf, the performance bar in the sport has been raised dramatically and permanently.

The idea of golfers as fitness buffs isn't especially surprising anymore. It's hard to remember a time when working out was considered a strange habit. Moreover, it was even discouraged. Golfers were once afraid that lifting weights would make them muscle-bound and ruin their swings. Various kinds of exercise were seen as impediments to performance, or as something that was simply unnecessary for better golf. Given the success that fit golfers have had and the prevalence of exercise in the sport today, it seems silly to us that anyone could undervalue it. Yet most players remain very ignorant of or at least resistant to nutrition. Which is potentially even more important than working out.

Think about what you see players eat on a golf course. For the most part, they eat the same foods bowlers and dart throwers eat — we're talking hot dogs and beer!

But "who cares?" you say. It's just golf, right? Why should you fuel up like a marathon runner or weightlifter when your sport never even gets you out of breath? Heck, you may not even break a sweat the whole round.

No one's judging you on how your body looks. Just how important could nutrition be?

The answer: much more important than you realize.

Golf takes a long time to play. The average round lasts about four to five hours and is usually spent under a hot sun. There's a lot that can happen in between shots. You may lose concentration, become tired, get angry after a bad shot, or develop muscle cramps. Believe it or not, all of these hazards are influenced by what you put in your mouth.

Hole-in-One Nutrition aims to accomplish two things: to make you aware of how eating poorly has been adding strokes to your game and to show you how simple changes can have you playing better golf in no time. **Hole-in-One Nutrition** will improve your game beyond what any expensive club, ball, coach, or sports psychologist can offer you. It's based on hard nutritional science, along with my own years of practical experience working with fitness-seekers and athletes of all kinds. Among these athletes are numerous amateur golfers, as well as PGA and LPGA touring professionals.

Part 1 is the "Why?" Why is nutrition important for golf performance? I'll give you a brief history of sports nutrition and introduce you to the **Hole-in-One Nutrition** pyramid.

Part 2 is about hydration, the foundation of all nutrition that goes way beyond just gulping water or Gatorade. Learn to master the balance of fluid and electrolytes in your body, and you'll never lack energy or focus on the course again.

Part 3 is about whole foods. Avoiding processed foods and choosing healthy ones is both critical to your playing ability and your overall long-term health and well-being. If you plan on playing golf until the day you die — and plan on doing it injury-free — you simply must make consuming natural, whole foods a priority in your life.

Part 4 of this book discusses supplements. I know you've seen, read about, probably tried, and are certainly confused about them, so I will demystify this topic once and for all. The short answer is that some supplements do work. I'll take you through the ones that are key for peak golf performance. These supplements will help you alleviate injuries and cramping and promote concentration and recovery.

Part 5 is the **Hole-in-One Nutrition** User's Guide. It's great to know about the importance of hydration, whole foods, and supplementation, but if you don't apply it, it's useless. Store this book in your golf bag. It should be as much a part of your game as your best driver, novelty club cover, or favorite ball mark.

ABOUT ME

I hold a postgraduate degree in Human Nutrition from the University of Bridgeport. I am a certified nutritionist and a certified strength and conditioning specialist and have been working in the fitness industry for over twenty years. I have worked with an array of athletes from the X-Games, UFC, MLB, NFL, NHL, PGA, and LPGA. My background in strength and conditioning gives me a unique perspective in regards to what an athlete's nutritional needs are for their sport. Since 2004, I've been the nutritionist for the Titleist Performance Institute (TPI) in Oceanside, California. This has given me the opportunity to work with a variety of players with many unique and different health problems or performance issues.

On a daily basis, I consult with players who are confused about what to eat for optimal performance on the course. A common statement is, "Rob, I'm so confused about nutrition. I don't know what to eat." Google has made it too easy to get information at your fingertips but not necessarily the right kind. This is what I call "paralysis with analysis," where golfers read too much information and are overloaded.

As a nutritionist and strength coach, I'm here to give sports nutrition an overhaul. I have the advantage of being in both worlds. Sometimes a new theory on protein may come out and be touted as new Holy Grail! Sometimes it may look good on paper but doesn't pan out on the course or in the gym. As you read on, I will give you evidence-based recommendations and "real world" evidence that I have personally gathered working with PGA and LPGA golfers and the average player.

PART I
Why Nutrition Is Important for Golf

1
NUTRITION
MADE SIMPLER

Playing eighteen holes typically takes around four hours, making golf one of the longest sports there is. It's one of the few sports where you can actually eat while you're playing. However, what you choose to eat will heavily influence how you feel and perform. Some of the recommendations I'm going to make in this book may surprise you and perhaps contradict what you already think you know about food and nutrition. Before I explain further, it's important to discuss what the popular thinking on nutrition (particularly for athletes) has been up to this point.

Sports nutrition has been heavily influenced by the United States Department of Agriculture (USDA) Food Pyramid. From its inception in 1992, the Pyramid served as the official, government-approved guidelines for healthy eating, and it was touted by registered dietitians and doctors for nearly two decades. In 2011 the USDA replaced the Pyramid with My Plate, an updated infographic. Despite the new My Plate, most of us were influenced by the Pyramid, so let's take a look at that first.

The old Food Pyramid promoted six to eleven daily servings of grains in the form of bread, cereal, rice, and pasta. The next level in the pyramid offered three to five servings of vegetables and two to four servings of fruit a day. Dairy and meat were limited to two to four servings a day. Fats and sugars (oils, sweets) were to be consumed as sparingly as possible.

If up to eleven servings of processed grains per day sounds insane to you — it flies in the face of most of today's popular diets, such as Paleo or Keto — you're correct: it was a terrible recommendation.

Due to new research and rising rates of obesity, diabetes, and heart disease, the Pyramid was changed in 1995 and later done away with in favor of My Plate, which limited grains to one-third of each meal and boosted the recommendation on vegetables. The USDA's intention was to get away from a one-size-fits-all approach and switch to encouraging people to eat healthy, but their message left many people confused about what and how much to eat. And my guess is you're one of them, and that's why I wrote this book.

I've simplified the science of healthy eating into a very basic food pyramid of my own called the **Hole-in-One Nutrition** Pyramid. It will help you play better golf, be leaner, and improve your overall health. When golfers follow it, the results are quick and amazing. Now let's dive in.

2
THE
HOLE-IN-ONE
NUTRITION PYRAMID

Keeping it simple is the best way to go about understanding and maintaining good nutrition. (For the record, is there anything that keeping it simple isn't good for? Except maybe rocket science?)

I break down the **Hole-in-One Nutrition** Pyramid into three levels.

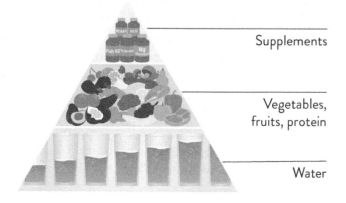

Supplements

Vegetables, fruits, protein

Water

The bottom tier, or base, of the **Hole-in-One Nutrition** Pyramid isn't exactly a food at all. It's water. The body is composed of up to 70% water. If hydration is not maintained, the body will suffer, and so will performance. Despite the fact that it's critically important, most people — even athletes — underestimate hydration. In fact, the only time I hear hydration emphasized among athletes is when they're performing in extreme hot and humid conditions.

It's important to realize that hydration is an issue when you're performing in moderate temperatures as well as in cold environments. You may have learned that staying hydrated is important for preventing muscle cramps. It is, but that's only the tip of the health and performance iceberg. Hydration will affect every single aspect of your game, from focus and concentration to hitting the ball farther off the tee. It simply has to be addressed first before we delve into the foods we eat.

The middle tier of the pyramid is whole foods — consuming food in the form it is found in nature. I have a personal story about my journey to discovering the value of whole foods. I hope it illustrates the power of whole foods and how you can benefit from them.

As a young athlete, I took part in every sport, from football, track, baseball, basketball, and skateboarding, to powerlifting. I was always looking for any edge I could get to increase my performance. I inherently knew that nutrition had to be part of that plan. I read fitness and bodybuilding magazines in the hopes of gaining knowledge of how to eat to become bigger, faster, and stronger. Of course, I came across ads by sports nutrition companies touting products that promised I would put on massive amounts of muscle, become shredded, and have endless energy.

I remember reading about a supplement that was supposed to increase muscle mass and strength rapidly. I was sold! It was the summer before my freshman year of football, and I desperately wanted to gain weight and increase my strength for the upcoming season. I went to GNC and spent a good chunk of what little money a fourteen-year-old boy has saved up to purchase the product.

The supplement instructions were to take a serving on an empty stomach before and after workouts. Unfortunately, I took the advice very literally, and since I didn't work out until the afternoon, I didn't eat for hours before I trained. My workouts were awful — without food, I had no energy, and the only thing I would fuel up with afterward was another scoop of the supplement. I ended up living on this product! And the most frustrating part of it was I never gained an ounce of muscle or saw any increase in strength. Nothing like what the bottle had promised. In fact, I actually lost progress.

My dad is a man of few words but is always full of wisdom. One day he saw my disappointment, and I remember him looking over to me and saying in his strong Korean accent: "Son, just eat real food."

It was simple yet straightforward. And he was right! The path to my goal had been in front of me all along.

Don't take the point of my story to be that all supplements are useless and a waste of money. Hold that thought. I'll come back to it in another chapter.

I just want to make it clear that whole foods come first, and a supplement is just that — a supplement to an already healthy eating regimen.

Believe me, once I started eating whole-food meals to support my workouts, my strength and muscle mass went through the roof.

"Just eat real food" should be the mantra of all golfers. Think of whole food as having a holistic effect on the body. (*Holos* is the Greek root that means "whole.") Whole food is food that is as close to its natural state as possible.

One example would be a baked potato, as opposed to instant mashed potato. Both are the same basic type of food, but a baked potato is in its whole state after cooking — it's still just a potato, only heated up. (Heated up just once, you'll note.) On the other hand, instant mashed potatoes have been processed. They've been cooked, with preservatives added to them, and are mixed by machines and poured into a container and covered with plastic. Eating instant mashed potatoes means you now have to heat them up again. Heating, processing, and reheating food breaks down the nutrients within it to a degree that it no longer offers the benefits a whole food does. A processed food is also known as a "refined food," and while that may make it sound like it's more sophisticated, it only means that you've stripped it of some of its best properties. You've made it worse for you.

The instant mashed potato, refined and processed, will result in unstable blood sugar when you eat it. That leads to low energy and excess inflammation. The chemicals used to preserve the food's shelf life are too controversial to explain thoroughly in this chapter, but suffice it to say they wouldn't be an issue if you had just gone with the baked potato.

Eating whole food creates a healthier golfer, which equates to quicker recovery times, increased energy, and less soreness after workouts. Making whole foods the majority of your diet is the key to your success on the course.

The third and final tier of my pyramid is supplements. To reiterate, whole foods are the foundation for supplements, and that's why they sit below them on the pyramid. If there's no foundation of whole foods, supplements don't work that well.

Supplements are much flashier and more aggressively marketed than whole foods, which explains why they stir up more questions from athletes. Some think that using supplements is not natural — that anything other than whole food is unnatural. On the flip side, there are other people that believe supplements represent the latest and greatest advances in nutrition science and therefore must have the edge on whole foods. And they're more convenient to boot, so why not load up on them?

Here's another quick story for you from when I consulted with a NHL player. On his first visit to my office, he pulled up and proceeded to open the trunk of his car. He emerged with an enormous box that few but a professional athlete could manage to carry and started walking to my office. He entered with the box, turning and angling it to pass it through the doorframe as if it were a piece of furniture. I asked him what was in it, and he opened the box to reveal what looked like the winnings of some fantastical *Charlie and the Chocolate Factory*-inspired contest: a lifetime supply of supplements. Or at least that's how it looked to me.

The hockey player only smiled and said, "Hold on. I've got more." He ran back to his car and pulled out — to my horror — another box of supplements of near-equal size.

Yes, his was an extreme case, but there are many out there (maybe you?) who think that supplements are more essential than whole foods. They will continue to miss out on the benefit of whole foods because they focus on buying the latest and greatest supplement.

There are thousands of supplements out there on the market. It's difficult to know which ones work best. I've used a multitude of supplements with many players. I know which supplements golfers can benefit from through research and real-world results.

Most of us are under a tremendous amount of stress, not just from the physical demands of exercise but also stress from the grind of daily life. Whenever you are stressed, physically and mentally, nutrients are depleted from your body. Nutrient depletions accumulate and lead to fatigue, inflammation, and incomplete recovery. When we discuss this tier of the pyramid, you'll finally learn the supplements that work for golfers.

Before we begin examining each tier of the **Hole-in-One Nutrition** Pyramid in depth, let me be clear that I don't expect you to drink the perfect amount of water, eat the most perfect foods, or buy every supplement on my list all the time. Instead, think of the 90/10 rule. If you do things right 90% of the time, you'll notice massive improvements in your body and on the course.

GEEK MOMENTS

And one last thing. I'm a bit of a geek when it comes to this nutrition stuff, so I'm going to have my geeky moments (my wife says I have a lot of these moments). Throughout the book, you'll see "GEEK MOMENT" sidebars and boxes indicating times when I'll geek out with research and a little scientific jargon. I've done my best to keep it simple and readable. I've always tried to give my players the reasoning behind every recommendation I make for them.

You don't HAVE to read the Geek Moments. They provide the "Why," but if you're only interested in the "How," the rest of the book has it covered.

PART 2
Hydration

3
WHY DRINK THAT CLEAR STUFF?

This is the most frequently asked question about water, from golfers and everyone else. Most people have seen the Gatorade commercials where athletes are sweating different colors from their pores. They give the impression that sports drinks must be better than water. So why drink this flat, flavorless beverage when there are so many more delicious options out there?

Sports drinks do contain water and electrolytes (not enough to impact electrolyte balance). They also contain a ton of sugar and other nasty ingredients that will affect your play on the course and your health. I'll discuss more on that topic later.

How important is water? Well, consider this. If you stopped eating food, you could survive for about three weeks, but if you don't drink water you can only survive for two to three days. Remember, the human body is composed of up to 70% water. The brain is made up of 85% water. By sheer volume, water is the most abundant macronutrient in the body. The amount of water your body uses to function is two to three liters per day.

Therefore, water must be replaced daily in order for the body to function normally. Water is used in every process in the body and has no reservoir to store it (in other words, drink up).

Most people walk around in a dehydrated state. They either don't drink enough water or they drink other fluids that have a diuretic effect, which dehydrate them further.

Proper hydration will help you:
- Make better decisions on the course
- Minimize muscle soreness after golf or your fitness routine
- Manage your stress on and off the course
- Maintain your ability to drive the ball farther
- Minimize joint pain

Water Is Thinkerade!

How many times have you heard about an athlete that has all the talent in the world and yet can't get it together on game day? People say "it's in his head" and assume it's a psychological barrier that may require counseling from a sports psychologist.

Well, maybe, but before embarking on some expensive therapy, the player should evaluate other factors that can affect the mental game. Cognitive function is a process by which one becomes aware of, perceives, or comprehends ideas. It's an ability to optimally and efficiently perceive, think, reason, and remember. In sports, cognitive functioning must be high when decisions must be made in a matter of a split second. Critical situations require focus and concentration to avoid mind clutter that could lead to a bad decision and a subsequent poor reaction.

Ask yourself this:
- Do I make careless mistakes during a round?
- Does my concentration start to fade toward the back nine?
- Do I make erratic and irrational decisions on the course?
- Do I say to myself, "Why did I make that stupid shot?!"

If you've answered yes to any of those questions, you could potentially resolve those mental mistakes with a simple ingredient: WATER! Good old H2O!

How many times have you forgotten where you placed your car keys? We tend to joke about brain farts like this, saying, "I must be getting older." In reality, the problem may be that the brain isn't getting the hydration it needs to run on all cylinders.

Research from the *Journal of Psychophysiology* has shown that a lack of water can cause a reduction of blood flow to the brain. Subjects were dehydrated by exposing them to increased heat or exercise on a treadmill. The dehydration resulted in impairment of short- and long-term memory, visuospatial function, perceptive discrimination, and reaction time — i.e., brain fog. Remember, the brain itself is made up of 85% water, so denying it water is like cutting part of it away! For this reason, I recommend that you drink water immediately when you wake up in the morning. This makes a massive difference in your energy and alertness and is the most effective thing you can do to clear brain fog.

Visuospatial function represents one of the brain's highest levels of visual processing. This is the ability of your brain to analyze the space around you, helping you understand distance and depth perception. This has a huge impact on your ability to hit a golf ball effectively.

Just how much dehydration do you have to suffer before you begin to lose brain function? The better question is how little. Most studies show that it only takes as little as 1–2 percent loss of body weight in water to impair cognition. In other words, a 150-pound player could start forgetting his golf clubs on the course after losing only 1–3 pounds of his weight in water — easy to do over the course of a round.

Of course, the amount of water a golfer loses is determined by the environment, pre-golf hydration levels, and the player's sweat rate. Some golfers look like they just hopped out of the shower when they walk off the course, and others don't look like they broke a sweat. One way to monitor your sweat loss is to weigh yourself before a round and then weigh yourself after the round. If you haven't lost any weight, you most likely hydrated properly. If the scale shows you dropped more than 1 percent of your body weight, you know to drink more water during the next round. Use this test, especially if you're playing in the heat. If you've lost weight, drink 8 ounces of water for every pound of water that was lost. That should help rehydrate you before your next round.

Water and Recovery

Most people consider golf a leisurely recreational activity that doesn't require much physical effort. However, golf does place a surprisingly high demand on the body. Paul Chek, author of *The Golf Biomechanic's Manual*, says an amateur golfer achieves approximately 90% of peak muscle activity when driving the ball off the tee. Imagine going to the gym and loading up a barbell with so much weight that you can only lift it three times.

That's the equivalent amount of energy and torque that is put on the body when you pull out your driver to nail your first shot.

All this energy and force puts the body into a catabolic state (tissue breakdown). Catabolism can be countered with anabolism (tissue buildup). These two processes are always in a delicate balance, but the net product should be anabolism.

Exercising is a catabolic process too. Training stresses the muscles, causing them to break down. Eating, resting, and other recovery measures allow the muscles to build back up bigger and stronger than they were. If you're practicing at the range and training in the gym to increase your driving distance and nothing is happening, you could be overtrained.

Signs of overtraining are:
- You hit a bad shot, and now it doesn't really bother you as much.
- A lack of motivation to go to the gym or play golf.
- Your body feels like you just finished BUD's training in the Navy SEALs.
- You suck down coffee and energy drinks to get through a round.
- No one wants to play with you because you're an irritable SOB!
- You find yourself on antibiotics every few months because you're sick.

Are you wondering where I'm going with all this? Wasn't I talking about water a few pages ago? Symptoms of overtraining can be reduced with the right amount of food and water. The catabolism that you create with practice and exercise can be controlled by what you put in your mouth. The journal the *Lancet* has shown that cellular hydration is an important factor in controlling cellular protein turnover. This means that when muscle cells are hydrated and swelling with water, there's an anabolic effect. As cells shrink with less water, they slip into catabolism. So walking around dehydrated is like asking to lose muscle. Drinking water will help hydrate your muscles, which will protect them.

It appears that stopping catabolism and starting anabolism is almost as easy as turning on a light switch. German researchers have shown that cellular hydration can change within minutes. This means that you're never too late to affect your recovery.

GEEK MOMENT: GLUTAMINE

 Glutamine is the most abundant amino acid found in skeletal muscle. It's considered a conditionally "essential" amino acid, meaning that the body can't make it on its own, so it must be obtained through food. Just as it is important for plants to have water for growth, muscles need glutamine to repair and recover. Golfers who train as hard as other athletes must have adequate glutamine in their diets.

I've already mentioned how dehydration breaks down muscle tissue. Research from the Lancet has shown that glutamine is released out of tissues that are in a state of dehydration. So not only does dehydration shrink the muscle cell and lead to tissue breakdown, it leaks gluta-mine from the muscles too. When you finish a workout, glutamine is there to help your muscles recover. But if you fail to stay hydrated, glutamine will leave your muscles and speed their breakdown, resulting in greater soreness.

The biggest mistake that golfers make is drinking a few beers after a round. Yes, a cold, refreshing drink feels great after a round, but it's the worst thing for your recovery. After you've played, your body is in a state of catabolism (muscle shrinkage). The sooner you stop the breakdown of muscle and start the repair process, the less sore you'll be the next day.

Drinking alcohol dehydrates you further because booze has a diuretic effect on the body, so it only pro-longs the time you spend in this catabolic state. Think of water as the spark plug for protein synthesis — the cat-alyst of an anabolic, muscle-building/recovering state. Water is the first ingredient for the rebuilding of muscle.

GEEK MOMENT: WHY YOU NEED TO BUILD MUSCLES

I've been writing a lot thus far about muscle gain and loss. If you're an older golfer, you may not think that muscles are important for you. You may think that wanting more muscle is simply for vanity. Something only for young players who want to show off their muscles. Nothing could be further from the truth.

Muscle mass is incredibly important for players of both genders and all ages, especially older folks. I'm sure you're aware of osteoporosis — the weakening of bones with age that predisposes a person to fractures if they fall. In the same way that bones become weak and brittle, muscles can shrink. The medical community refers to this condition as sarcopenia. As a person ages, muscle mass decreases. You may weigh the same at fifty as you did at thirty, but unless you've been strength training, your body composition is not the same and you carry less muscle than you did twenty years ago.

I remember consulting with a golfer who was sixty-three years old. I asked him about his weight and he said, "My weight hasn't changed since I was eighteen. I've been 187 pounds my entire life." I asked, "Do you look the same as you did when you were twenty?" He said, "Of course not! I've got this belly now!"

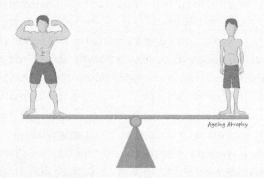

Ageing Atrophy

This is the result of a change in body composition. The "belly" means this client traded in muscle for fat. The loss of muscle mass will occur extensively in specific muscles, in particular the glutes, legs, and arms. These muscles are important for power and distance off the tee.

Muscle mass is also crucial for maintaining your metabolism, which in turn helps keep body fat levels in check. The more muscle mass you have, the more protection your joints have surrounding them during a fall. Furthermore, studies have shown that during exercise, the more muscle mass you have, the greater release of anabolic hormones that help you recover. Researchers from the Journal of Osteoporosis International referred to the loss of muscle mass through aging as aging atrophy. This atrophy mainly occurs in a very specific part of the muscle, the Type II fibers, also called fast-twitch muscle fibers. Fast-twitch fibers are the ones that help you to run fast, jump high, lift heavy things, and, of course, help you hit the ball far.

Water and food are important components to maintaining muscles, but exercise is an integral part as well. You have to perform exercises that load the body to cause enough stress for the muscles and bones to adapt over time. The best activity for muscle growth and bone density is resistance exercise in the form of strength training. Note that this doesn't automatically mean lifting weights. Using your own body weight for resistance or working with a suspension trainer or bands can also do the job.

The Pinball Effect

I always emphasize health when writing nutrition plans for my golf clients. First and foremost, I want them to be able to play golf well into their eighties. To do that, I have to minimize what I call the pinball effect.

Think back to the days when you played pinball. The object of the game is to make the ball hit as many targets as possible. The more targets you hit, the higher your score. There's a similar game going on in your body, but in this context, a high score is a bad thing.

The pinballs bouncing around inside of you are called free radicals — unstable molecules that ricochet through your body, hitting targets in an effort to become stable. The only way free radicals become stable is by taking energy away from other tissues in your body. When this happens, the tissues are damaged.

In this world, we're surrounded by free radicals. They're generated from pesticides we unintentionally inhale, herbicides we accidentally consume, medications, junk food, and even good, necessary things like exercise and the air we breathe. Dealing with free radical damage is part of the natural process of the body, and it's ready for it, provided you give your body what it needs to keep up in the game.

You may have heard of antioxidants. They're predominately found in vegetables and fruit (including vitamins C and E) and have been proven to help control free radical damage. There's another antioxidant you consume every day but are probably still deficient in. I bet you'll never guess what it is ... water.

GEEK MOMENT: WATER AND YOUR DNA.

 Researchers from Yonsei University in Seoul, South Korea, investigated hydration's effect on oxidative DNA damage and exercise performance. Subjects were divided into four experimental groups:

Group 1:   A control group (nothing was changed).
Group 2:   Subjects were dehydrated in a sauna with no rehydration.
Group 3:   Subjects were dehydrated in a sauna but given water before the exercise protocol.
Group 4:   Subjects were dehydrated in a sauna but given a sports drink before the exercise protocol.

All of the groups worked out, running on a treadmill to exhaustion. Blood levels of malondialdehyde (MDA, a marker of oxidative stress from free radicals, were measured before training. MDA levels turned out to be higher pre-exercise in the dehydrated groups versus the control group. In addition, total antioxidant status (TAS), a measure of how active antioxidants were in the subjects' bodies, were lower in the dehydrated groups versus the control. In other words, being dehydrated when you work out wreaks havoc on the body.

Researchers concluded that dehydration increases DNA damage and impairs exercise performance. Groups 3 and 4 that rehydrated with water or a sports drink alleviated oxidative damage. It's worth noting that water was just as effective as a sports drink in preventing the pinball effect.

Water comes first for antioxidant protection. If you are dehydrated because you forgot to drink enough water, don't give up. The Korean study discussed above showed that even in a dehydrated state, drinking water reduced free radical damage and enhanced recovery after exercise.

Stress Reliever

Hormones go way beyond testosterone and estrogen. One hormone that can affect every part of your body is cortisol. The adrenal glands are about the size of a walnut and sit right above the kidneys. Whenever you're stressed, cortisol is produced by the adrenal glands to manage stress. We tend to think of stress as being mentally or emotionally taxing; it's physically draining too. The time you spend on the course or in the gym is a form of stress.

Think of cortisol as the ultimate multitasker in the body. Dr. James Wilson, author of *Adrenal Fatigue*, discusses cortisol's many functions:

- blood sugar regulation
- immune response modification
- heart and blood vessel toning
- central nervous system stimulation
- stress reaction normalization
- anti-inflammatory effects

There are times when your cortisol levels may be high to deal with stress. That's normal, although levels should revert back to a physiological level after the stress is gone. You want just enough. I always test cortisol levels in all my players. In many cases, they're in a state of dysfunction.

GEEK MOMENT: THE CORTISOL RHYTHM IN YOUR BODY

Cortisol is a stress hormone. Every time you're stressed out, the adrenal glands produce cortisol as part of your "fight or flight" response, so you have the energy and focus to protect yourself. But that's not the only time that cortisol plays a role. Cortisol is a diurnal hormone.

This means it should be released in high amounts in the morning and lower amounts in the evening. When the sun starts to rise, cortisol is the hormone that says "get out of bed." It acts like a sort of internal coffee drip.

The International Journal of Psychology refers to the rise of cortisol within twenty to thirty minutes of waking as the cortisol awakening response (CAR). But even before you wake up, cortisol levels are on the rise. When you sleep, cortisol levels are at their lowest point. During the second half of your night's sleep, they'll begin to rise and peak when the sun comes up.

When your cortisol rhythm is off, other hormones get out of whack too. Cortisol's opposing hormone is melatonin. This is the hormone that helps you fall asleep at night. In a dysfunctional cortisol rhythm, cortisol levels are low in the morning and high in the evening, which is the opposite of what they should be. The consequence of low cortisol levels in the morning is a golfer who presses the snooze bar several times and doesn't want to get out of bed.

On the other hand, elevated cortisol levels at night make it difficult for a golfer to fall asleep. Good sleep habits are essential for maintaining a good cortisol rhythm, which in turn promotes better energy to make your early-morning tee times.

If cortisol levels are dysfunctional, it can affect your body's ability to combat inflammation. You've probably heard of athletes or golfer friends of yours being injected with a cortisone shot to fight wrist or shoulder pain. This is done to control inflammation. When cortisol levels are low or dysfunctional, there's not enough cortisol to go around, and injuries feel worse.

Remember that stress comes in many forms. Excessive training can be a massive stress to the body. So can skipping meals, as well as making poor food choices. All of these instances tax your adrenals and call on them for cortisol.

Management of cortisol is necessary for recovery. As a stress hormone, cortisol is released when the body has its "fight-or-flight" response. If a tiger should suddenly run onto the green while you're putting (or an alligator, if you're playing in Florida), cortisol will help you get away from it. It does this by breaking down tissues such as muscle to create energy for your legs and arms. Preserving muscle is not a priority of the body. Creating energy so you can fight the tiger or run away is the priority.

So cortisol puts you into a temporary state of catabolism. This is fine when stressful situations demand it, but chronically elevated cortisol levels cause the body to continually break down tissue.

US Army research has shown that a lack of water can cause hypercortisolemia, which is excess production of cortisol. Not properly hydrating on and off the course is an added stress to the system. Even in times of dehydration, drinking water has been shown to normalize cortisol levels. So if you haven't hydrated properly before stepping on the course, it's never too late to start. Grab a water bottle.

The Ultimate Post-Workout Recovery Drink

During and after you exercise, there is a soup of hormones stirring up inside your body. These hormones impact inflammation and recovery. As mentioned earlier, cortisol can be an anti-inflammatory hormone. Cortisol levels that are too low can leave you in a state of inflammation, while excess cortisol causes excessive catabolism. One hormone that counteracts cortisol is testosterone.

GEEK MOMENT: EXERCISE AND HORMONES

 Your body's hormonal response to exercise depends on the type of exercise that is performed. Testosterone and growth hormone — both anabolic hormones — are released when the intensity of your exercise is high. High-intensity exercise is any activity that lasts from ten to forty seconds at a very high effort.

These are some examples:
- Thirty-second sprints on a bicycle
- Thirty-second sprints on a treadmill
- Lifting weights with loads that restrict you to six to twelve reps

After finishing a set of high-intensity exercise, you should be sucking air. That is a sign that the effort was high enough that the body will produce testosterone and growth hormone. Since exercise is a stress to the body, cortisol is also produced, along with testosterone.

Research from the University of Jyväskylä, Finland, has determined that the higher the ratio of testosterone to cortisol (T:C), the faster you recover from exercise. In the context of hydration and exercise, the Journal of Applied Physiology has shown that dehydration increases cortisol postexercise and attenuates the production of testosterone.

You know that testosterone is an anabolic hormone. It calls for the construction of new tissue. You generally want as much of it as you can (naturally) produce, whether you're male or female. Optimizing testosterone levels after exercise is a big boon to recovery, and being dehydrated can spoil it by lessening the release of testosterone and letting more cortisol spill out.

To get the most of your workouts, whatever type you do, be fully hydrated beforehand.

Power Aid

Finishing strong at the end of a match is so important. Old Dominion University researchers looked at the effects of dehydration on a one-repetition maximum bench press with weight-trained males. They tested how much the subjects could bench one time then dehydrated the men in a sauna for two hours. Afterward, scientists retested the men's bench presses.

They lost only 1.5 percent of their body weight in the sauna, but the subjects' bench-press performance decreased dramatically. After rest and rehydration, they tested their maxes a third time, and their lifts went back up to predehydration levels.

This study applies to golfers. Players often tell me that they lose distance on their shots as a match goes on. This is partially due to the fact that the player is becoming dehydrated during the round, especially in hot climates. Think of how many matches are lost in the last few holes due to fatigue and weakness. Proper hydration will help the player maintain strength and distance off the tee.

4
THOW TO STAY HYDRATED

Now that I've made my case for why hydration is important, the question is how will you stay hydrated in the real world — and on the course? How much water is enough?

The most common recommendation for water intake is eight glasses per day. This is a good starting point, but recommendations should be individualized to take into account the varying size and weight of different people. For example, if a female weighs 100 pounds, drinking eight glasses of water may be too much for her to get down. On the other hand, a 200-pound man will quickly find that eight glasses falls far below what he needs.

To determine the optimal water intake for your body, use this formula that I learned from Dr. F. Batmanghelidj's book, *Your Body's Many Cries for Water*: drink half your body weight (in pounds) in ounces every day.

180 lbs ÷ 2 = 90 ounces of H_2O

Body weight	Water per day
150 pounds	75 ounces
200 pounds	100 ounces
250 pounds	125 ounces

What About Other Fluids?

When I say you need to drink water, I mean you need to drink water. Other fluids don't count toward your total daily intake. To be very clear, the following drinks do not count as water:

1. coffee
2. tea
3. soda
4. energy drinks
5. juices
6. milk
7. sports drinks
8. flavored water
9. alcoholic beverages

If you're a person who only drinks coffee, juices, and tea for your hydration, cutting back to plain water may sound extreme and impossible. I think Dr. Batmanghelidj says it best when it comes to other fluids besides water:

"In advanced societies, thinking that tea, coffee, alcohol, and manufactured beverages are desirable substitutes for the purely natural water needs of the daily 'stressed' body is an elementary but catastrophic mistake."

You can still enjoy those beverages as long as you drink the right amount of water first. Not only can you do it, but you'll love it too. The reason plain water is optimal over other liquids is fluid absorption. A simple example of other fluids affecting hydration is the sports drinks commonly used in endurance sports. Marathon runners tend to dilute carbohydrate drinks like Gatorade by half or even more because of the high sugar content. They know that if they don't dilute the carbs, it'll sit in the stomach and cause potential GI problems during the race. The same holds true for juices and soda.

Timing of Water Intake

Timing, as they say, is everything. There is no exception with drinking water. The most important time for drinking water is in the morning. Many people like to hop on the scale in the morning because they weigh less. Unfortunately, it's not because you lost fat overnight but because you're dehydrated. Your weight may fluctuate one to four pounds overnight.

It's critical to drink water right when you get up due to the loss of water during sleep. Notice I said water and not coffee. You may be the type that stumbles toward the coffee maker first thing in the morning, fumbling for the "on" button, but you should be reaching for a glass of water instead.

Please understand that waking up groggy isn't normal. Life doesn't need to be like that. What your body wants is water. Whenever an athlete takes my advice on this, brain fog clears, energy increases, and the desire for coffee is less.

Sound nice? Read on!

Look, I like coffee too (especially a nice espresso). I'm not asking you to stop drinking it. That's why my motto is "water first, then coffee." Once your main hydration base is covered, you can drink other liquids with relative impunity.

I suggest that you drink 25% of your total water intake in the morning. Below are some examples of the amounts you'd need, depending on body weight.

Bodyweight	Water per day	Water upon rising
150 pounds	75 ounces	20 ounces (2.5 cups)
200 pounds	100 ounces	25 ounces (3 cups)
250 pounds	125 ounces	32 ounces (4 cups)

You may be saying "Whoa, Robert! That is a lot of water!" But in the grand scheme of hydration, it's not that much. Compare three 8-ounce glasses of water to a Venti from Starbucks. Most people have no problem sucking that thing down, so how could drinking water be that hard?

A major benefit of getting in the bulk of your water first thing is that you'll sleep better at night. I find that most people back-load their water intake, meaning they drink most of their water toward the evening. That becomes a problem because they'll wake up in the middle of the night to pee and sometimes can't fall back asleep. You should be sleeping through the night uninterrupted, and shifting your water to the beginning of the day helps tremendously.

So how do you do this? Ultimately, you must create a habit in order to be consistent. Before going to bed, most of you have a routine, closing the windows, locking the doors, and turning off the lights. I want you to add one more to that routine. Grab a water bottle or stainless steel canteen. Fill it with water and a pinch of unrefined sea salt (more on what this is later) and place it next to your alarm clock.

When you wake up in the morning, the first thing you will see is your bottle, and you'll be reminded to drink. Chug it, sip it, or swirl it in your mouth like it's fine wine. Just drink it.

During Activity

Fifty percent of your total water intake for the day should be consumed during your golf round. Due to stress and potentially extreme environmental conditions on the course, refueling with water is most critical during this portion of the day. See the chart below for estimates of how much you need.

Bodyweight	Water in Ounces Per Day	Water during a round
150 pounds	75 ounces	37 ounces (4.5 cups)
200 pounds	100 ounces	50 ounces (6 cups)
250 pounds	125 ounces	64 ounces (8 cups)

DO NOT USE THIRST AS AN INDICATION OF HYDRATION LEVELS. If you wait to feel thirsty, you're already dehydrated and suffering the consequences. If it's not a golf or workout day, spread out your water intake throughout the day.

GEEK MOMENT: THE PARADOX OF EXERCISE AND THIRST

 Logically, you would think that most people drink more water during exercise when they're sweating and exerting themselves, but research shows this isn't always the case. University of Illinois researchers call it "voluntary dehydration." Even with free access to water, most people do not drink enough to hydrate themselves. In fact, it was found that subjects were only replacing a third to two-thirds of their water loss during exercise.

Don't rely on thirst for the signal to hydrate. Stay ahead of the game and drink water throughout your workout or activity whenever possible, whether you feel like it or not.

The Rest of the Day

The remaining 25% of your water consumption should be consumed throughout the day and around meals. You don't want to wait till you sit down to eat to drink water exclusively. If you find yourself gulping water during a meal, you may not be chewing your food adequately.

GEEK MOMENT: STOP CHEWING YOUR FOOD LIKE A DOG

I have a boxer named Gia. If a dog could be a foodie, she's it. Any time I give her a piece of meat, she inhales it. No chewing, just bite and swallow. Just like Gia, many people don't chew their food. That's fine for a dog, but when I see people take huge bites of food, chew a few times, and then choke it down, I shake my head. People who don't chew their food thoroughly drink tons of water during a meal. This is done by instinct to help push the food down so it doesn't get stuck. Unfortunately, it's a poor substitute.

Chewing your food is the first step to better digestion. The best example that I've heard to illustrate the value of chewing belongs to Dr. Alan Gaby, an expert on nutritional medicine. He gives the example of a pile of ice chips and a block of ice in the sun. As you can imagine, the ice chips in the sun will melt faster than the block of ice because they've been reduced to smaller, more manageable components. In the same way, food that is broken down first, like ice chips, will go on to be more easily digested than food that is swallowed near whole.

There's another great quote I love from Mahatma Gandhi: "Drink your food and eat your drink." "Drink your food" means we should chew our food thoroughly until it is liquid before swallowing. Think of chewing your food as a cement mixer. Each time you chew, you're mixing saliva with your food and turning it into a pulp that can easily slide down your throat for the next step in the digestive process. Chewing is especially important with regards to carbohydrate digestion. Your saliva contains amylase, an enzyme that breaks down carbohydrates. The more you chew, the more the carbohydrate is broken down. Failure to chew properly means amylase can't do its job, and you can suffer bloating, belching, and indigestion as a consequence.

Types of Water

It's funny to think something as elemental and common-place as water has become so complicated. Nowadays, there are so many types of water: flavored water, fortified water, bottled spring water, pH water... Which is best?

First, avoid flavored waters. There should be no sugar or artificial sweeteners added to your water. The truth is, if you feel the need to drink fluids with bubbles in it or something sweet, you're dehydrated, plain and simple. Once the proper amount of water is consumed, the need for carbonation or flavor quickly dissipates. It may seem impossible, but give it time. I bet you you'll reach a point where your diet soda doesn't taste so good anymore.

Another big trend right now is pH water, or alkaline water. Some people are actually paying thousands of dollars for some kind of unit that can increase the pH of their water. They often report they feel better when they drink it, but my take is that it's the first time in their lives that they're drinking enough water! Until further research comes out, I'm not fully convinced that pH water is the best water to consume.

GEEK MOMENT: PH WATER CAN BE BAD FOR YOU

 Drinking too much pH water could be detrimental to your health. Let me explain. One day I received a text from one of my players on the PGA tour. He was complaining about his digestion. More specifically, he had complaints of bloating and indigestion after meals. This player eats very well, and I was a bit perplexed by his sudden digestive issues.

After talking with him, I discovered he made one change. He started drinking high-pH water.

It's important to understand pH and how it impacts the body. A pH scale measures the relative acidity-alkalinity of a substance. The pH scale ranges from 0 (most acidic) to 14 (most alkaline). A pH of 7 is considered neutral. In general, the blood tends to be slightly alkaline (pH 7.4). Due to this fact, most people think the entire body should be alkaline. This is partially true. However, the stomach should be acidic (pH 1–3). The acidity is important for several reasons. One is protection for the gut. Think of acid as chlorine. If you accidentally swallow a parasite or bacteria, the acid kills it so that it doesn't pass into the other parts of the digestive tract. Second, acid helps the absorption of key vitamins and minerals such as B vitamins, calcium, and iron. Lastly, acid is critical for protein breakdown and absorption.

When acidity is low in the stomach, the chief symptom is indigestion and bloating. The PGA player lowered the acidity of his stomach by drinking high-pH water before meals. This compromised his digestion of protein, which led to the indigestion and bloating. Once I had him stop the high-pH water, his digestive system normalized.

The most important aspect of water is that it's clean. It should taste clean so that you enjoy drinking it.

Bottled and Filtered Water

There are pros and cons when it comes to bottled water. Some of the concerns with bottled water are the environmental impact, cost, taste, and purity. My biggest worry about it is the purity. The bottled water industry is a multibillion-dollar business. It's inevitable that some companies will cut corners in search of bigger profits.

In 2011, the Environmental Working Group (EWG) released a bottled water report, grading waters according to:

1. Source. Did the company give the geographical water source on the label?
2. Treatment method. How was it determined to be safe, and is this explained on the label?
3. Purity. Does the company post its purity test results online?

According to EWG, 50% of the waters on the market are NOT filtered and may contain bacteria, parasites, chlorine, and other chemicals. Claims such as the water is "from pristine sources" were bogus. Many times, bottled water is taken straight out of the tap.

Companies that indicate the mineral content of their water tend to be the higher-quality waters. They will have a breakdown of the minerals in the water. For example:

Mineral	Amount (mg/l)
Chloride	6.8
Calcium	80.0
Nitrates	3.7
Magnesium	26.0
Sulphates	12.6
Sodium	6.5
Bicarbonates	360.0
Potassium	1.0
Silica	15.0

These waters may be more expensive, but in my opinion, you get what you pay for. If you're going to consume bottled waters, choose ones that have approximately 200–300 parts per million (mg/L) of total dissolved solids (TDS). Martin Fox, Ph.D., author of *Healthy Water for a Longer Life*, says that this amount ensures health and proper hydration. Examples of high-quality bottled waters are Evian, Fiji, Mountain Valley Spring, and Trinity.

If you choose to buy a filter to run your water through at home, reverse osmosis filters are very good at filtering out bacteria and chemicals, but they pull out some of the good stuff too, such as calcium and magnesium. Since the TDS is low, the water is bare in minerals. Water with a low TDS will cause the body to expel water to maintain the mineral balance the body already has, so it may cause you to run to the bathroom more often.

A great way to remedy this situation is to add a small pinch of unrefined sea salt to every liter of water (about four cups, or 33 ounces) you drink. Unrefined sea salt contains trace minerals. When I say a small pinch, I mean it. It shouldn't be enough to change the taste of your water. If it tastes like seawater, you put way too much in.

Some people find that adding a touch of unrefined sea salt to water makes it more palatable and allows them to drink more with enjoyment.

Tap water quality will vary where you live. Chemicals such as chlorine and fluoride can be added to the water supply, which can be harmful. In addition, heavy metals such as lead may be present from old pipes. For these reasons, I would recommend you filter your water before drinking out of the tap. Reverse osmosis filters can be expensive if you buy them, but you can rent filtration units for an affordable price. A Berkey filter is one of the best filters you can buy. They have systems that range from 1.5 to 6 gallons.

The Natural Electrolyte

Whenever the word "electrolyte" comes up, we think of Gatorade and other sports drinks. These beverages do contain electrolytes but in insufficient quantities to have any meaningful impact. They also contain massive amounts of sugar and other toxic ingredients. These are some of the electrolytes that are found in your body:

- sodium
- potassium
- chloride
- calcium
- magnesium
- bicarbonate
- phosphate
- sulfate

Electrolytes are nutrients in your body that regulate important functions such as heartbeat and muscle contraction. Most people are unaware that eating salt supplies electrolytes. You've probably been told to avoid salt because "it's bad for your health," but the reality is that you need salt, especially when you sweat.

You've probably tasted your own sweat by accident on more than one occasion. Salty, isn't it? Sweating drains you not just of water but also of electrolytes, and both must be replaced for the sake of recovery.

Imagine exercising and having someone collect every bit of sweat that is pouring out of your body. Believe it or not, this has actually been done. After collecting the sweat, researchers analyzed it and found that, of all the electrolytes, sodium was the most abundant.

Therefore, you need to consume salt with your water. A lack of salt may lead to cramping. In extreme cases, athletes will go into a massive cramping episode similar to their body going into rigor mortis.

On the flip side, athletes can drink too much water and ingest too little salt. Hyponatremia is a condition in cases where an individual has overconsumed water, which has diluted the salts in the body. This puts the body in electrolyte imbalance. It tends to happen to marathon runners. In extreme cases it can be fatal.

Think of your blood as needing the same consistency as ocean water. The body's fluid is referred to as our "inner ocean."

A common scenario is a player who hits the links on a humid summer day. The player's natural inclination is to drink a ton of water to stay hydrated, but doing so without salt leads to an imbalance in the inner ocean, because water is being replaced without electrolytes. This may lead to mental fatigue, lethargy, and cramping.

A simple solution is to add unrefined sea salt to the water. Unrefined sea salt is completely different from white table salt you see in kitchens and restaurants. We have all grown up to recognize salt as white. But real salt is not white. In fact, unrefined sea salt looks dirty!

White salt has been heated and treated with chemicals to extract the other mineral salts so that it looks pretty and pure to the consumer. Unrefined sea salt has not been altered in any way. In other words, the salt has not been exposed to chemicals, heat, or solvents. Dr. David Brownstein, the author of *Salt Your Way to Health*, says that the unrefined sea salt brand has been shown to have over eighty trace minerals.

By using unrefined sea salt, you not only replace salt in your body but other minerals as well. Simply adding a small pinch of unrefined sea salt to your water helps maintain hydration levels and prevent dehydration.

I know you're probably concerned about salt consumption and high blood pressure. Dr. Mark Houston, director of the Hypertension Institute and Vascular Biology of Nashville, says it's completely safe to consume unrefined sea salt, even when someone has high blood pressure and takes medication. Refined salt, on the other hand, is toxic to the body. Regular white salt is only sodium chloride. So if you only consume this salt, it can adversely affect blood pressure.

Table salt is like white bread. It's been stripped of the nutrition for the sake of making it look pure and pretty. unrefined sea salt, in comparison to regular salt, looks dirty because other minerals such as magnesium and potassium are present in it. This is a good thing.

I know I said that white salt is toxic. It's not completely forbidden. Let's say you're running late to a tee time and forget to hydrate properly in the morning. It's extremely hot and humid, and you're sweating more than normal. As the round progresses, you begin to feel lightheaded and notice slight cramping in your muscles.

You drink more water, but the symptoms worsen. Your calf cramps into a ball, and you can't walk another step. I've had some players in this situation. It's ideal to have unrefined sea salt, but any salt is necessary at this point, since your body is depleted. Add regular salt to your water or eat anything that's salty, such as potato chips or salty peanuts. It's not ideal, but it's the best strategy in the situation.

Putting the Lid on Water

Water is probably the most underrated source of nutrition on the planet. It's the foundation for performance in all activities. If you don't have enough water in your system, you don't have the raw ingredients to support brain function, strength, hormone production, and recovery. Drink half your body weight in ounces per day and add a pinch of unrefined sea salt to every liter of water you drink. Give it two weeks, and you'll notice big differences in how you feel and perform.

5
FAQS ABOUT WATER

If I increase my water intake, won't I be peeing all day?

At first, the "urge" may come on more frequently. There is always an adjustment period that occurs when you change anything about the way you eat or drink. So give it a bit of time — up to two weeks.

If you are still running off to the toilet at that point, it could be how you are drinking. If you are chugging your water like you're in a beer contest, slow down. Sip water throughout the day. This will help slow down the urge.

Another solution can be adding minerals to your water. As mentioned earlier, bottled and filtered water are often very bare in minerals. Remember your inner ocean. Increasing your water intake without minerals makes the body feel as if its ocean is being diluted. In an effort to maintain homeostasis (balance), the body will try to get rid of the extra water by making you pee. To restore the mineral balance, add a pinch of unrefined sea salt to every liter of water you drink. This ought to fix it.

Water has no taste! Can't I drink flavored water?

Cravings for sweet or carbonated water are a sign that you are dehydrated. Believe me, when you start drinking enough water, they'll go away.

I had a client who was overweight and living on diet soda. I'm talking three Big Gulps per day. At 28 ounces of diet soda per Big Gulp, that's almost 90 ounces of diet soda per day!

At 250 pounds, this gentleman needed to consume 125 ounces of water per day. When he heard me say that, his eyes grew as big as golf balls! He said, "Rob, this is impossible! Water has no taste, and I don't think I can do it."

Since this was such a radical change for him, I told him to simply drink three Big Gulps' worth of water — the same amount of liquid we both knew he was used to. I told him that after he got through those, he could continue to drink as much diet soda as he wanted, but the water was the first priority.

It took him about three weeks to get the hang of it, but after that, something interesting happened. He came in one day and said he had been drinking the three Big Gulps' worth of water but stopped drinking the diet soda. I told him he could still drink diet soda if he wanted, but he said he no longer wanted to. "After three weeks of drinking water, I went to get a Big Gulp, but when I took a sip, it tasted like chemicals. I thought there was something wrong with the machine. So I bought a can of diet soda, and it tasted the same. Soda just didn't taste the same to me anymore, so I stopped drinking it."

This kind of reaction happens quite often. Just drink your allotment of water for the day and see what happens.

What about sports drinks?

Sports drinks contain water and electrolytes, but they also have sugar. A lot of sugar. Seventeen grams per every eight ounces in some cases. Most sports drinks are sold in sixteen-ounce bottles. On average, golfers will consume one or two bottles during a round, adding up to a whopping 68 grams of sugar! You'll never burn that off in a round of golf.

Sugar raises your blood sugar levels, which jacks up your insulin, which leads to energy crashes. You'll end up feeling tired, fatigued, irritable, and, eventually, fat.

I worked with an NFL player who told me that as a kid he dreamed of making the pros and being sponsored by Gatorade so he could drink as much as he wanted. Once he turned pro and was on an NFL roster, that dream came true. He had access to Gatorade all day during training camps and during the season. At first, he was in heaven. There were refrigerators full of all types and flavors of Gatorade at his fingertips. He drank one before morning practice, during his workouts, and on his way home.

The problem was he noticed that he was getting a gut. Even doing two-a-day workouts, he couldn't stop his stomach from growing. I had to point out that his weight gain was due to the sugar in the Gatorade. When he got off the stuff, he lost the gut. I know what you're thinking: *I'll just drink G2.* Even though G2 has low sugar, it has insufficient amounts of electrolytes to make any difference and many artificial ingredients. So stay away from the sports drinks!

I heard that ice water will increase my metabolism. Is that true?

Consuming ice water has been shown to increase metabolism due to the fact that the body has to warm up the water in the stomach before it can assimilate it. The body burns calories to help warm up the water. This can be a useful weight-loss strategy but may not be such a good choice for optimal hydration before and during golf.

Your body can't use ice-cold water immediately. It must first warm up the water before it can be absorbed. This warming process takes time. Therefore, the hydration process will be slowed. When you're on the course on a hot day, you need water to get to your cells quickly. Ice water will slow absorption. Slightly chilled water or room temperature water is better for quick hydration.

If I had to choose between diet soda and regular soda, which one is better for me?

Imagine I have a driver in one hand and a seven iron in the other hand. With which one do you want to get hit over the head? Whether it's diet soda or regular soda, it's going to hurt your body. The main difference between the two is the sweetener.

Diet sodas are usually sweetened by aspartame. Research in the *Journal of Applied Nutrition* has shown that aspartame has many potential side effects such as:

- headaches
- neuropathy (weakness, numbness, or pain from nerve damage)
- vision issues

- tinnitus
- dizziness
- confusion
- severe drowsiness and sleepiness
- tingling, pins and needles, or numbness of limbs
- depression
- anxiety
- severe insomnia
- heart palpitations
- nausea
- diarrhea
- abdominal pain
- skin issues
- aggravation of allergies
- precipitation of diabetes
- severe joint pain
- depressed immune system

Those are only twenty out of 551 symptoms in this one report.

Once aspartame is consumed, it's broken down into other chemicals that act as a neurotoxin. A neurotoxin is a poison to the nervous system. The chemical by-products from aspartame attack the nerves. Realize that the nervous system is what controls your muscles, so aspartame could be affecting your ability to swing a golf club.

Some people that become hooked on diet sodas have a very difficult time giving them up. Aspartame has been argued to have addictive properties, which has huge implications for weight gain. Many people that are overweight drink diet soda because it is calorie-free. The thought is that since there is no sugar and calories, there will be no weight gain. But University of York researchers showed that just the taste of sweetness even without calories from artificial sweeteners still stimulates the same processes in the brain as if you ate sugar. The end result is your body thinks it has eaten sugar, and hormones are released to handle that sugar. This creates a hormonal milieu that promotes weight gain, despite the lack of extra calories being present.

Diabolical, I know. And unfair.

So if you're an overweight golfer and need to lose a few pounds, it's probably wise to stay away from diet sodas.

Nevertheless, there is a new generation of sodas that are sweetened with stevia, a sweetener that comes from a shrub. The active ingredient is a crystalline compound called stevioside. It has no calories and is 100–300 times sweeter than table sugar. You'd think it would create the same weight-gaining effect as other diet sodas that contain no calories. However, its action in the body appears to be different. Brazilian researchers have shown that stevia actually lowers blood glucose, which can reduce the risk of diabetes. So, in light of this, I'm not dead set against diet sodas that are sweetened with stevia, but I still want you to drink your allowance of water first.

And what about regular soda? It's typically sweetened by high-fructose corn syrup (HFCS), which isn't any more natural than what's in most diet options. It's a sugar that has a significant amount of fructose versus regular table sugar. Since it has a different chemical makeup, it reacts differently in your body.

Researchers at the University of Fribourg, Switzerland, studied the effect of HFCS on blood pressure. They gave subjects 60 grams of sugar in two separate drinks. One group was given glucose and the second group was given HFCS. Even though overall sugar consumption was the same in the HFCS group and the glucose group, the HFCS group experienced an increase in blood pressure in the short term.

The scary part about HFCS is the long-term effect on the body. In the *Journal of Circulation*, researchers performed a long-term study on over 6,000 middle-aged subjects over four years. They wanted to know if the consumption of soda affected metabolic syndrome (MetS), a prediabetic condition. These are a few signs of the development of MetS. Your belt size begins to creep up over several years. At your yearly checkup, your doctor tells you that your blood pressure is starting to creep up. If at that same appointment the doctor says your fasting glucose is above 100 mg/dL, the development of MetS is very insidious. As with any disease, it doesn't happen overnight. The researchers showed that less than a can per day increases your risk of developing MetS and eventually diabetes. This is why I recommend that you don't drink regular soda as an easy way to lower your chances of MetS or diabetes.

I heard that if the color of my urine is clear, I'm well hydrated. True?

The color of your urine is not an indicator of hydration. It may seem that the clearer the urine, the more hydrated you are. But this is thrown off if you take any vitamins. For instance, B2 (riboflavin) has a bright yellow appearance in the urine. I know what you're thinking: "I've got expensive urine." Some think this is the case when it comes to B vitamins and vitamins. Just because you see it in the urine, that doesn't mean your body is not using it. It simply means that your body is excreting what it doesn't need. Not everything you eat gets completely absorbed. That's why you have stool and urine. You still eat protein, carbohydrates, and fat. Your body uses what it can and eliminates what it can't use. It's the same way with vitamins.

If you're taking B vitamins, there's no need to increase your water until it's clear. Use the guideline of half your body weight in ounces to stay hydrated.

I'm confused about coffee. Is it healthy? Safe?

The research can be confusing. Some research says it's great for diabetes, whereas another study says it's not.

I have simple guidelines when it comes to coffee. There are three situations when you may need to rethink your morning cup of Joe. First, if you have stomach issues, coffee is out. The acids in coffee tend to exacerbate conditions such as reflux, bloating, and gas. Once you heal your gut, you may be able go back to coffee. Second, if you have sleep issues, coffee should be off the menu. Sleep issues include the inability to fall asleep, waking up in the middle of the night, and waking up feeling unrested. If you normally have coffee in the afternoons, try having a cut-off time of noon. The half-life of caffeine is about six hours, so having your last cup of coffee at noon gives the body a chance to eliminate the caffeine.

Lastly, if you are a zombie without a cup of coffee, it may mean that you've formed a dependence on it and should take a break from the caffeine for a while to reac-climate yourself.

Caffeine withdrawal from coffee can be a horrible thing. I wouldn't recommend going cold turkey unless you're up for headaches and lethargy, but you should begin to cut down.

Before reducing coffee, make sure to drink half your body weight in ounces of water with unrefined sea salt.

This will help prevent some of the side effects of withdrawal. Take it slow. If you consume three cups of coffee per day, reduce it to two per day for a week and then one cup per day for a week. After a cup for a week, have coffee every other day and decaf on the other days. Soon enough you'll find that you don't need coffee, and energy levels will be back to normal.

Is drinking out of plastic water bottles dangerous?

Plastic contains a chemical called bisphenol A (BPA). This chemical is classified as a xenoestrogen, which means it's similar to estrogen in the human body. Think of this chemical like a knock-off Titleist driver made in China. It looks the same and feels the same but doesn't perform the same. BPA has been shown to disrupt the hormonal system in both men and women.

Do the best you can to drink your own water at home. If you do have to drink out of plastic water bottles, avoid leaving your water bottles in the car. When you heat up plastic, the BPA levels increase dramatically. Many people buy huge packs of water bottles and leave them in the trunk of their car, which is a sure-fire way to consume a bunch of xenoestrogens.

Does mineral water count toward my total water intake for the day?

Mineral water can be a great source of minerals, since the total of dissolved solids is quite high. Yes, mineral water does count toward your total intake for the day. Drink 80% of your intake as plain water and the remaining 20% as mineral water. However, if you tend to belch after drinking it, refrain from drinking it during a round of golf. The constant belching could disrupt your game.

PART 3
Whole Foods

6
WHEN FLATLINING
IS NOT A BAD THING

If you were to look at an electrocardiogram (ECG) of your heart, you would see a graph that looks like a roller coaster. The line will have peaks and valleys — a good sign that your heart is still beating and you're alive and kicking. But if the graph flatlines, you're dead.

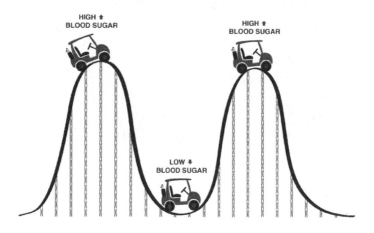

When it comes to graphing your blood sugar, you want just the opposite of a healthy ECG. If your blood sugar rises and falls sharply, your energy, mood, and strength will be just as erratic.

You'll feel like you're on a roller coaster.

If your blood sugar drops too low or climbs too high, that's a stress on your body. You have hormones that are on high alert to handle it, but at a price. Keeping your blood sugar flatlining is the key to athletic performance and good health. Insulin and cortisol are two of these hormones. Every time blood sugar goes up, insulin is released to bring it down, and when it's low, cortisol brings it up — at the cost of muscle tissue (see the Geek Moment sidebar below).

GEEK MOMENT: THE BOUNCER'S JOB

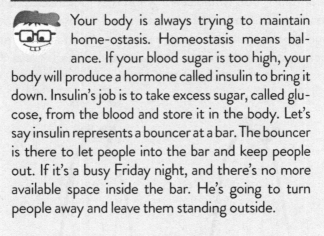 Your body is always trying to maintain home-ostasis. Homeostasis means balance. If your blood sugar is too high, your body will produce a hormone called insulin to bring it down. Insulin's job is to take excess sugar, called glucose, from the blood and store it in the body. Let's say insulin represents a bouncer at a bar. The bouncer is there to let people into the bar and keep people out. If it's a busy Friday night, and there's no more available space inside the bar. He's going to turn people away and leave them standing outside.

Insulin works in much the same way, shuttling sugar from the blood into the liver and muscles. But when they're at full capacity, insulin has no place for the glucose to go. It will shuttle it into your fat cells like a bouncer tosses miscreants into the street. And that, in a nutshell, is the obesity problem we have in America.

Constantly elevated blood sugar exhausts insulin and your body's capacity to store the sugar in the best places. Instead, it gets stored as fat. On the flip side, if your blood sugar drops too low, cortisol is produced. If you remember from the previous chapters, cortisol is a hormone that is produced by the adrenal glands. Cortisol breaks down tissue, including your hard-earned muscle, to provide energy. If you don't eat for a long time, allowing your blood sugar to tank, your body perceives this as a threat to your life. It releases cortisol to raise your blood sugar back up, and it does so by harvesting muscle. This happens in a matter of seconds.

When you hear reports of tiny women lifting cars off their trapped children, that's the adrenal glands kicking in adrenaline and cortisol to provide tremendous energy. That's how fast your body works to increase glucose in the system in emergency situations. It's best to leave this process for emergencies only. You're not supposed to use it on a regular basis because you'll break down your muscle.

So, to sum up, too much blood sugar means more insulin and gaining fat. Too little means more cortisol and losing muscle. Keeping your blood sugar on an even keel is the sweet spot that keeps you lean and healthy.

Think of cortisol in particular as your personal assistant. If you ask him to get you a cup of coffee, and he spends all his time researching where to get you the best one, he's not getting all the other tasks you assigned him done. When you waste cortisol on managing your blood sugar rather than performing its many other functions, there are consequences (see the Geek Moment on this page).

GEEK MOMENT: CORTISOL AND JOINTS

We all have our priorities. Our body has priorities as well. Its main job is to maintain blood sugar levels. As mentioned earlier, cortisol has many jobs in the body. Another job of cortisol is to manage inflammation in achy joints. If you don't flatline your blood sugar, you will have exhausted your supply of cortisol. The absence of cortisol won't be able to act in reducing the inflammation in a joint.

When a golfer fails to control blood sugar, the cortisol that could help deal with injuries is directed to solve the blood sugar problem. The way your body views it, losing a joint is acceptable; dying due to a lack of energy is not. The result is that your aches and pains will take longer to heal.

Years ago, I was contacted by an amateur golfer. He wanted to consult with me for a chronic shoulder problem. At this time, my schedule was full, so the earliest I could see him was in two weeks. In the meantime, I had this player change his diet. He skipped breakfast or ate cereal in the morning and only drank a few cups of water each day. I had him eat a hardboiled egg in the morning with an apple and increased his water intake to half his body weight in ounces.

The two weeks had passed, and I saw this player. As I started the interview process, I asked him how his shoulder was doing. He said, "I have no shoulder pain." I was a bit perplexed. I asked him, "Didn't you contact me because of shoulder pain?" He said, "Yes, I did, but once you changed my diet, the shoulder pain went away!" This is a common scenario with many of the players I work with. Controlling blood sugar in turn manages cortisol so it can help deal with inflammation.

Mom Was Right, Eat Breakfast

We've heard it before. "Breakfast is the most important meal of the day... You must eat breakfast before you take the test/play the game/leave for work... Breakfast gives you energy." Mom was right when she made these recommendations.

When you get up in the morning, you're coming out of a fasted state. Due to fasting for eight hours, your blood sugar is low. Whatever you choose to eat or drink at this time will impact your blood sugar for the rest of the day. It's a critical window of opportunity — an opportunity to flatline your blood sugar and create an environment for long-lasting energy, focus, and strength throughout a round of golf.

If you skip breakfast or eat foods that put you on a blood sugar roller coaster, you blow the opportunity. Breakfast can make or break you.

You may not eat breakfast. You may not like it or think you have time for it. But if you don't eat it, it will negatively affect the rest of your day. If you're the kind of person who slips into a food coma after lunch, listen up.

In nutrition research, there is an effect called the second-meal phenomenon. Ana Jovanovic, a scientist at Newcastle University, has demonstrated that eating breakfast controls blood sugar after lunch. In this study, one group of subjects were given nothing for breakfast, and another group were given breakfast. They gave each group the same lunch then measured everyone's glucose levels after lunch.

The subjects who ate breakfast had a "73% reduction of blood glucose" after eating lunch. That means the breakfast eaters enjoyed steadier blood sugar, which translates to more energy. The reason you fall into a food coma after a meal is the rapid rise and then fall of blood sugar after you eat lunch. Simply eating breakfast can prevent this rise and fall and preserve your energy well into the afternoon and evening.

You may be saying to yourself, "I play in the afternoon, so this doesn't apply to me." However, it's very important for the player with an afternoon tee time. The second-meal phenomenon shows that eating breakfast will help control blood sugar after lunch. Therefore, it's critical you eat a good breakfast to ensure you have stable blood glucose before an afternoon round of golf.

The Older Player

You may think that low energy and declining memory is inevitable and that it's just part of the aging process. I've got good news for you. It doesn't have to be. University of Toronto researchers took subjects ranging from sixty-one to seventy-nine years old and had them fast overnight. All subjects were given four different breakfasts on four different days. The breakfasts were divided into a placebo (nothing), carbohydrate, protein, and fat group. The carbo-hydrate, protein, and fat group showed memory enhance-ment, but the no breakfast group did not. So your age doesn't matter. You can always improve memory, espe-cially by eating breakfast.

Breakfast of Champions

Now that you know skipping breakfast is not an option, let's discuss what to eat for breakfast. You may think that a cereal like Wheaties is your best option. I cer-tainly believed it as a kid growing up. It's hard not to believe it when you have sport icons like MJ and Mary Lou Retton on the front of the box.

Well, I hate to break it to you but ...

Cereal is the absolute worst food to eat for breakfast!

I know that this may go against everything you have heard. Nevertheless, cereal is toxic. It's undergone pro-cessing, which removes the nutrition from the whole grain. Processing leaves it a pile of mostly empty (nutri-tionally devoid) calories — albeit crunchy, tasty ones. See the "cereal is toxic" Geek Moment for a full explanation.

GEEK MOMENT: CEREAL IS TOXIC

 There is an interesting study discussed in a book titled Fighting the Food Giants, by Paul A. Stitt. He was a biochemist that worked in the food industry. While working for Quaker, he came across a report of a study in which four sets of rats were given four different diets.

- One group of rats received plain whole wheat, water, vitamins, and minerals.
- The second group received puffed wheat, water, and the same nutrients as the whole-wheat group.
- The third group was given water and white sugar.
- The fourth group was given water, vitamins, and minerals.

Here are the results:

The rats that received the whole wheat lived over a year. The rats that received nothing but water, vitamins, and minerals lived about eight weeks. The group fed white sugar and water lived for a month, and the rats given vitamins, water, and all the puffed wheat they wanted died in two weeks!

According to Stitt, the reason the puffed wheat group died so fast is due to the processing of cereal. The grain is put under 1,500 pounds of pressure in order to give it that crunch that we all love. Stitt concluded that the rats didn't die of malnutrition but rather from the puffed wheat itself. He thought that the puffed wheat was nutritious before processing but was now a toxic substance.

The process that Stitt referred to is called extrusion. University of Maine researchers showed that there are chemical changes that occur with extrusion. This is a quote from the study: "Proteins, starches, and non-starch polysaccharides can fragment, creating reactive molecules that may form new linkages not found in nature."

And therein lies the problem. If you can't find it in nature, don't eat it. This is why whole foods are part of my food pyramid, and cereal is not.

Don't be fooled by slick packaging on cereal labels. Since there has been a movement toward whole foods in the food industry, many cereals will have labeling saying that it's "made from whole grains." This is certainly true. The cereal was made from food that was at one time a whole grain. Now that it's crunchy, it's no longer a whole grain. What it will do to your blood sugar isn't worth the few vitamins and minerals your body can get from it.

My Experiment with Cereal

Try this. Go to your cabinet, grab a box of cereal, and put a handful in your mouth. I did this with Rice Krispies.

I chewed five times and then let the cereal sit in my mouth. It took all of sixty seconds for it to turn to mush.

The digestion of carbohydrates starts in your mouth. Your saliva contains amylase, an enzyme that breaks down carbs — particularly the kind of carbs found in cereal. Imagine taking a bite of an apple and chewing five times. It won't break down that easily. This is what keeps blood sugar stable and why apples are a better food choice than cereal.

The faster a food digests, the faster your blood sugar spikes. Whenever there is a peak, there is a valley to follow. The reason why cereal digests so fast is because of extrusion — the processing that makes whole grains into crunchy cereal flakes. All cereals, even the "healthy" ones, go through extrusion and send you on the ultimate blood sugar roller coaster ride.

7
PFF: PROTEIN, FAT, AND FIBER

You've heard of "BFF": best friends forever. When it comes to flatlining your blood sugar, your BFF is PFF: protein, fat, and fiber. These are the three best foods for stabilizing your blood sugar and being a healthier, better golfer.

Protein Power

I'm a big fan of protein. I've been a fan since I was a teenager. I always ate a lot of protein, because my ultimate goal was to get bigger and stronger for sports like football. At the time, that was all I knew about protein — that it helped you build muscle.

Since my teenage years, I have come to appreciate the fact that protein is important on many other levels. Protein is one of the most important nutrients to the human body. In fact, the word comes from the Greek word *proteos*, which means "of primary importance." Every single cell in your body is made of protein.

The protein you eat eventually breaks down into amino acids. There are twenty different amino acids. Nine of these are considered "essential," which means your body can't make them on its own. You have to eat them to get their benefits. Amino acids are responsible for:

- Increasing your focus and concentration
- Repairing your tissues
- Increasing your energy
- Optimizing your hormones
- Boosting your metabolism
- Maintaining and building lean body mass

There is a pool of amino acids in the body that is drawn upon daily by the body. Amino acids replace enzymes and hormones and are for general wear and tear. Even if you're sedentary, you need protein on a daily basis. The need for protein increases when you're more active, playing golf, and/or working out.

Brain Food

A common problem among golfers is the inability to concentrate and focus. This can lead to making irrational decisions. Said another way, it can lead to getting pissed off after a bad shot. These may be signs that you need more protein for a better mental game.

Amino acids are the precursor to neurotransmitters, which are chemical messengers that allow signals to transmit from one neuron (nerve cell) to another. Julia Ross, author of *The Diet Cure*, describes neurotransmitters as brain chemicals that can create certain moods. She classifies these neurotransmitters into four types.

Neurotransmitter	Effect on body
Dopamine, Norepinephrine	Natural caffeine
Gamma amino butyric acid (GABA	Natural sedative
Endorphin	Natural painkiller
Serotonin	Natural mood stabilizer and sleep promoter

As you can see, amino acids are responsible for some powerful chemicals. Dopamine and norepinephrine are the neurotransmitters that are key to your focus and concentration on the golf course. Don't think that a cup of coffee in the morning is enough to get you through a round. Your body has the natural ability to produce the focus and alertness you need to perform your best — if you give it what it needs.

GEEK MOMENT: THE TRUE 5-HOUR ENERGY

 The Harvard School of Medicine has shown that the consumption of protein increases dopamine. Subjects in one study were fed 60 grams of canned tuna, and their dopamine levels were examined every thirty minutes for five hours. As it turned out, the subjects' dopamine remained elevated for the entire length of time. A single meal of tuna gave them sustained energy.

You must eat a significant amount of protein daily, starting with breakfast. This will help produce the neurotransmitters you need to focus, delay fatigue, and increase work output when you play.

Tissue Repair

These days, golfers are incorporating more types of training into their programs. It could be weight training, Pilates, sprinting, or endurance training. All exercise puts the body in a state of catabolism. Catabolism, if you recall, is a breaking down of tissue. You don't get stronger in the gym — you get stronger recovering from the damage you did to your muscles in the gym. That's why the "more is better" idea is a dangerous line of thinking when it comes to physical training. No matter what training you do, you have to ask yourself how much you can handle. You can only recover when you stop catabolism and reverse it with proper nutrition and rest.

One of the classic signs that a golfer is not recovering efficiently is constant soreness. Muscle soreness after weight training is normal, especially if you have started a new routine. If soreness persists for days after a workout, it usually means that recovery is not optimal.

This can be a big problem for a golfer. Take, for example, a female player who needs upper-body strength to improve her power off the tee. She is motivated and trains really hard to improve her upper-body strength. But there's just one problem: she can't lift her arms after training. I have seen this many times with golfers who are trying to build strength or power. The training is affecting the practice of their sport, which hurts their skills and ultimately defeats the purpose.

GEEK MOMENT: DOMS

 Let's says you've just finished a killer leg workout. Your legs feel a bit shaky but you're okay.

The next day rolls around, and to your surprise you feel a slight soreness. You're thinking that it wasn't so bad — you could have gone harder. But on the morning of the second day, you can't get out of bed. Your legs are stiff as a board and ache like they've been hit with a bat. What happened? DOMS happened. Delayed Onset Muscle Soreness.

Your muscle fibers are made up of actin and myosin. These protein filaments slide across each other to contract muscles. Think of these actin and myosin filaments like a thick rope. If you were to slice a rope, it would look very similar to a cross-section of your muscle. Think of DOMS as the rope being stressed to such a degree that the fibers of the rope start to fray because of all the tension that's put on it. In the same way, when you perform hard workouts, you cause this fraying action on the actin and myosin filaments. This is damage to the muscle on a microscopic level. That's the source of your soreness, but as I'm sure you've noticed, it's temporary. It may take a day or two to set in (hence the "delayed onset"), but it will dissipate on its own. The appropriate amount of protein will help minimize DOMS and speed recovery.

Mauro Di Pasquale, M.D., the author of *Amino Acids and Proteins for the Athlete : The Anabolic Edge*, says, "Exercise suppresses protein synthesis [muscle growth] and stimulates protein degradation in muscle in proportion to the level of exertion of the athlete."

In other words, the more training and practice you perform, the more catabolism occurs. Therefore, the protein needs of the athlete are high.

I have analyzed hundreds of food journals from athletes from all sports. It doesn't matter if it's a weekend warrior or a pro athlete, most do not eat enough protein. The lack of protein is the number one cause of muscle breakdown in athletes, and simply eating more protein throughout the day will do wonders for your recuperative abilities.

GEEK MOMENT: GAGS

 Joint recovery is just as important as muscle recovery. You may have heard of glucosamine sulfate. It has been shown to help with arthritis and chronic joint issues by giving the body the raw materials to help regenerate the joints. It does this by helping to produce glycoaminoglycans (GAGS). Think of GAGS as food for your joints. Notice that the word glycoaminoglycan has "amino" in it. The only way your body can make GAGS is if you give it amino acids, which come from proteins. If you don't eat enough protein, your body can't make GAGS, and your joints will suffer.

Optimization of Hormones

Performance-enhancing drugs (PEDS) are always a hot topic in sports. Many professional athletes take drugs to improve recovery, increase muscle mass, lose body fat, and enhance performance. And make no mistake — they work. But as with any drug, side effects are inevitable. The most common drugs used are derivatives of testosterone and growth hormone.

Guess what? Your body produces testosterone and growth hormone. You can optimize the production by eating the right foods. You won't raise your hormones to the level that you'd get from injections. However, you can make great gains without risking your health (or breaking the law) by improving your diet.

Danish researchers conducted a study to determine the effects of a high-protein diet versus a high-carbohydrate diet on short-term hormone output. Subjects followed meal plans for both diets respectively. The high-carbohydrate diet produced growth hormone, but when the subjects ate more protein, their growth hormone climbed highest. So, if you want to increase growth hormone, put down that bagel and grab a turkey drumstick instead.

Another way for you to maximize hormone production is to exercise regularly. Lifting weights in particular increases the production of testosterone and growth hormone.

GEEK MOMENT: AN EXERCISE IN TESTOSTERONE

 One of the best ways to naturally boost testosterone levels is exercise, but not just any kind. Here are some rules you must follow to raise it.

Pump some iron
William Kraemer, Ph.D., of the Exercise Physiology division of US Army Research, has found that there is an elevation of anabolic hormones during resistance training. Variables such as intensity of the exercise and amount of muscle mass used to perform it are important. Intensity refers to the loads you lift. You should perform strength exercises in the six to ten rep range and strive to push heavier weights in that range over time. Of course, technique must be perfect with these types of loads.

In addition to higher intensities, you should choose exercises that use big muscle groups. For instance, an exercise such as a squat activates more muscle in the legs (and upper body too) than a leg extension machine. If you want to train with just your body weight — which is fine — pull-ups, push-ups, and lunges can give your hormones a boost.

Limit endurance training
You read that right. Unless you're an endurance athlete — and a golfer isn't — endurance training

should not be a big part of your physical fitness regimen. Yes, it's true that a round of golf may take four to five hours to play, but the activity itself is stop-and-go. You perform quick bursts of speed and power throughout the game (i.e., swinging the club). Long, slow endurance exercise, such as jogging or cycling, will not help your speed and power.

On the other hand, if you're not sure about your cardiovascular (CV) fitness, test yourself. Chris Maund, an expert in endurance training, says you should have a base of CV fitness. At minimum, you should be able to walk up three flights of stairs without becoming winded. If you find yourself gasping for air at the top of three flights of stairs, this is a sign you need some CV fitness training. If this is the case, incorporate one to two sessions a week of slow, steady state cardio for thirty minutes to create a base of cardiovascular fitness.

If you've got a base of CV fitness, then repeated intervals of short-burst training should make up the majority of the cardiovascular exercise you do for golf. In the European Journal of Applied Physiology, research has shown that endurance athletes have lower testosterone levels due to the duration of their running. Look at the physiques of Lance Armstrong and Usain Bolt. It's not hard to see who the more powerful athlete is.

Short and sweet

More is not better when it comes to the length of your training sessions. If you train hard for too long a time, you can end up lowering your testosterone and growth hormone levels, leaving you worse off than when you started. A good general rule is to limit your workouts to an hour. If you're in the gym longer than that, you're probably spending too much time socializing!

Increase Metabolism

Your metabolism refers to the way your body processes energy. None of us are getting any younger. We want to maintain or increase our metabolisms for our health, our waistlines, or our golf game.

Carrying around a lot of extra weight isn't just unhealthy and unsightly; it hurts your ability to swing a club. Excess weight negatively affects your ability to create speed and power. Think about the quickest and most powerful football players. They are always the running backs, wide receivers, and defensive backs. Most of these players have washboard abs!

I'm not saying you have to have washboard abs to be a great golfer or a fit person. But the lower your body fat, the less dead weight will be hanging around to slow down your swing. Boosting your metabolism and losing weight will also result in your getting less fatigued on the course (especially if you carry your own bag).

One easy way to raise your metabolism? Eat more protein!

GEEK MOMENT: EAT FOOD TO BURN FOOD

 The mere act of eating food can burn off calories and raise your metabolism. In scientific terms, we refer to this as the thermic effect of food (TEF). The period of time after you eat is called the post-prandial period. During this time, your body uses energy to break down, absorb, and store the food you eat. Dutch researchers have shown that the body uses more calories performing these processes with protein than it does with carbohydrates and fats. In fact, protein requires up to four times more calories to deal with than carbohydrates and twenty times more calories than fat. The message is clear: eat more protein and you'll burn more calories.

Increase Lean Body Mass (LBM)

Lean body mass essentially means muscle mass. Whenever the word "muscle" is mentioned, some golfers get scared. It conjures up images of Arnold Schwarzenegger and other muscle-bound men. You have to realize that it takes a lot more than a few workouts and drinking protein shakes to look like Arnold. It takes years of dedicated training with the goal of being a bodybuilder to turn into one. It doesn't happen by accident.

Most people don't even have the genes to be as big as a bodybuilder. And, truth be told, many bodybuilders enhance their already rare genetics with "special supplements" that are neither legal nor safe. Don't worry, this book won't take you down that road.

Muscle mass helps a player. Look at most of the long-drive champions. Rarely are they little lanky guys. They're some big dudes! The more muscle mass you have, the further you can hit the ball. It's a simple physics equation: force = mass x acceleration. Obviously, maximizing the acceleration of the club will provide more force, but another way is by adding mass. Putting more mass on your glutes, legs, and back helps produce power off the tee.

If you're an overweight golfer, muscle mass will help you, too. Think of muscle as an engine. What burns more fuel, a Lamborghini or a Camry? The bigger the engine, the more fuel burned. A bigger engine in your body means more calories burned and fewer that can be stored as fat.

Muscle mass is really important for older athletes too. As early as age twenty, muscle mass begins to slowly decline. When you lose it in the glutes, legs, and back, which are the major power sources for sports, you lose distance on your shots. The loss of muscle mass in these areas will predispose you to injury in the lower back and shoulders.

Studies performed with healthy Italian centenarians concluded that the more muscle mass they maintained, the healthier and more functional they were late in life. Eating protein is a big part of maintaining and building muscle mass. So, from now on, think of protein not just as a muscle builder but also as nature's ultimate anti-aging food.

Be Satisfied

The last thing you want to distract you during a match is hunger. I consulted with a professional athlete who was constantly hungry. He would eat breakfast and still be ravenous during practice. During the middle of practice, he would reach into his gym bag and grab handfuls of nuts to stave off the hunger. It got to be so distracting during practice that the coach had him contact me to check for digestive issues.

After analyzing his food journal, it was clear that he was not eating enough protein. His breakfast was all carbohydrates. He thought that was okay, since carbohydrates provide energy. Too bad he didn't know about the blood sugar roller coaster (remember the ECG we discussed earlier?) Once he started eating an adequate amount of protein, he was no longer famished. Eating a high-protein breakfast — think eggs and oatmeal rather than breakfast cereal or a muffin — will stave off feelings of hunger so you can concentrate on the course.

Q Squared

Hopefully, I've convinced you by now that you should be eating protein for myriad health and performance reasons. But there are some things you should be aware of when you increase your protein intake. When it comes to protein, think of Q squared.

- Quantity
- Quality

Quantity

Since there is no reservoir for amino acids in the body, you must eat protein daily and throughout the day. Make sure to eat protein at every meal. Remember that protein comes from the Greek word *t*: of first importance. Your first priority when you compose your plate of food is to focus on protein you can put on it. I'll discuss specific amounts later in the book.

Quality

I'm a big believer in beef, chicken, pork, fish, and shellfish. Basically, any animal food is going to supply good-quality protein. Animal protein contains all the amino acids that are considered "essential."

GEEK MOMENT: BCAAS

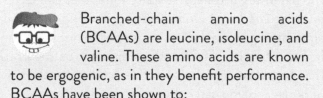 Branched-chain amino acids (BCAAs) are leucine, isoleucine, and valine. These amino acids are known to be ergogenic, as in they benefit performance. BCAAs have been shown to:

- increase protein synthesis
- reduce postexercise soreness
- increases focus and concentration
- burn fat
- increase muscle mass

There is one caveat: BCAAs are predominately found in only one type of protein — animals. There is a massive difference between the protein found in animal meat and non-animal sources (plants). Dr. Loren Cordain, author of The Paleo Diet for Athletes, says that 1,000 calories of lean meat supplies 33.6 grams of BCAAs, whereas 1,000 calories of whole-grain supplies a measly 6 grams of BCAAs. There's no contest when it comes to the type of protein that is best for a golfer. Meat makes the meal. The difference between the protein found in animal meat and non-animal sources (plants). Dr. Loren Cordain, author of The Paleo Diet for Athletes, says that 1,000 calories of lean meat supplies 33.6 grams of BCAAs, whereas 1,000 calories of whole-grain supplies a measly 6 grams of BCAAs. There's no contest when it comes to the type of protein that is best for a golfer. Meat makes the meal.

Are You a Thoroughbred?

If you owned a horse that will race in the Kentucky Derby, do you feed it the cheapest food source, or do you find the best-quality hay and alfalfa for it? Obviously, you would buy the highest-quality food to make the most of your investment. Think of yourself as a thoroughbred. Invest in yourself. Seek out the best quality protein sources available. When it comes to eating meat, always try to eat the best quality you can.

	Beef	Chicken	Fish
Best	Pasture/Grass fed beef	Free-range organic chicken	Wild fish
OK	Organic beef (grain-fed beef)	Conventional raised chicken	Sustainably farm raised fish
Worse	Processed canned meats (i.e Spam)	Chicken nuggets	Fried catfish

Artemis Simopoulos, an expert in omega-3 fatty acids, has shown that eggs from pasture-fed chickens have significantly more omega-3s than conventionally raised eggs. You'll find out later how important omega-3s are for your health and for performance. For now, take note that free-range food is superior to food that comes from an industrial feedlot.

8
FAT IS YOUR FRIEND

When I think about how our society views fat these days, I think of the old adage: "A lie told often enough becomes the truth." Eating fat has been demonized and condemned. It's been blamed for heart disease, diabetes, high blood pressure, and obesity. And while you've heard these accusations for decades — maybe your entire life — none of them are true.

First, we were told that cholesterol was bad for you and that we should avoid eggs. Then we were ordered to avoid all saturated fat, so we switched to eating more vegetable oils (such as in margarine and canola oil) because they were supposed to be healthier.

Most recently, the scientific community dropped another bomb and told us only trans fats are killing people. So if you're confused about what fats are, what they do, and whether they're safe or the scourge of the earth, I don't blame you.

Most experts now agree that we need some fats to be healthy. Every single cell in your body has fat in it, and fat is essential for the function of each one of those cells. Sally Fallon, author of *Nourishing Traditions*, says fat plays a role in:

- cell membrane health
- energy
- carrying vitamins to cells
- mineral absorption
- hormones
- blood sugar control
- controlling inflammation
- fat burning
- satiety

The mainstream nutrition motto on fat nowadays is eat "healthy fats" and avoid the "bad fats." But what exactly is a healthy fat? And what's a bad fat?

First off, we have to know how fats are classified before we can praise or condemn any fat. Fats can be monounsaturated, polyunsaturated, or saturated. But even these classifications are flawed because foods don't fall cleanly into one category.

Dr. Mary Enig, author of *Know Your Fats*, says, "The practice of calling animal fats 'saturated' is not only misleading, it is just plain wrong. For example, beef fat is 54% unsaturated, lard is 60% unsaturated, and chicken fat is about 70% unsaturated. This makes these animal fats less than half saturated. Therefore, they really should be called unsaturated fats. In fact, none of the naturally occurring fats and oils is made up of only all saturated or all unsaturated fatty acids; rather, they are mixtures of different amounts of various fatty acids."

If calling animal fats "saturated" is incorrect, then avoiding them on the basis that they're saturated is not only foolish — it's impossible.

Whole foods that contain fat are made up of a blend of fats. So while an egg contains saturated fat, it also contains other fats, including omega-3s, omega-6s, and monounsaturated fats such as oleic acid. Oleic acid is widely regarded as a "healthy" fat that is also found in olive oil and almonds.

GEEK MOMENT: CHICKENS ARE WHAT THEY EAT

 When you go to buy eggs, consider the chicken they came from. What the chicken eats is important. Dutch researchers showed that the type of fat in an egg changes depending on what the hen that produced it eats.

Researchers separated chickens into three groups. One group was fed groundnuts (peanuts). The second group was fed soybeans. The third group was fed linseed (flax seeds). The chickens fed peanuts ultimately had a higher oleic acid content, while the chickens fed soybeans had a higher omega-6 content. The chickens fed linseed had more omega-3s. Ideally, you want to eat an egg that's higher in omega-3s.

Research where your eggs come from and choose eggs from chickens that have been fed flax seed over those that have been fed soybeans.

Think about what the fat is in the animals it comes from. A chicken grows from the yolk of an egg — the white surrounding it is the protein that nourishes it, while the yolk itself is mostly fat. When you throw away an egg yolk, it's like you're throwing away a chicken. You're losing the most valuable part of the egg.

Saturated Fats Are Not the Villain

What if I told you to only eat salads and avoid all the cruciferous vegetables such as broccoli, cauliflower, Brussels sprouts, and cabbage? You'd think I was a lousy nutritionist, and you'd be right. It would be idiotic to cut out cruciferous veggies, because they contain so many healthy nutrients. Saying you should only eat monounsaturated and polyunsaturated fats is just as ridiculous.

One study that appeared in the *American Journal of Clinical Nutrition* had healthy subjects divide into three groups. Each was randomly assigned a diet that featured only palm oil, coconut oil, or olive oil for its fat sources. Palm oil and coconut oil are classified as saturated fats and are therefore considered by most nutritionists to be the "bad fats." Olive oil is classified as monounsaturated fat and is generally considered a "good fat." All three groups were fed similar macronutrient profiles (amounts of protein, fat, and carbs); only the type of fat was different.

The results showed that there were no differences in the effects on plasma homocysteine, TNF-alpha, IL-1-beta, IL-6, highly sensitive C-reactive protein, and interferon-gamma.

And what does all that mean in English?!

All the markers tested are indicators of possible signs of cardiovascular disease and inflammation. If saturated fats were half as bad as they've been made out to be, the groups that were given palm oil and coconut oil should have fared far worse than the olive oil group — but they didn't. The bottom line: saturated fats do not cause an increase in risk factors for heart disease.

Guilt By Association

The misinformation about saturated fats and chronic disease goes back to the old Food Pyramid again. The USDA Food Pyramid told us to avoid fats that are solid at room temperature. Trans fatty acids such as margarine and shortening are solid at room temperature, but so are saturated fats like butter, lard, tallow, and coconut oil.

The difference is that butter, lard, tallow, and coconut oil are found in nature, while trans fats have been chemically altered.

The industrial process that produces trans fatty acids is called partial hydrogenation. Liquid fat is converted into a solid fat. Although saturated fats and trans fats are both solid at room temperature, they are completely different fats on a chemical level.

We have to be very careful with research that indicates saturated fats are bad and cause disease. In most cases, trans fats are grouped together with saturated fats in the experiments. Therefore, when trans fats are found to be dangerous, saturated fats often get the blame too.

The Case for Cholesterol

Most foods that have saturated fats also have some cholesterol as well. To the same degree that saturated fat is necessary for the body, cholesterol is just as important for good health.

Sally Fallon, author of *Nourishing Traditions*, says cholesterol is important for:

- cell membrane integrity
- hormone production
- bile production
- Vitamin D production
- tissue healing
- nerve conduction

Research from Saudi Arabia showed that decreasing cholesterol in the diet was not a factor in predicting a heart attack. Rather, reducing HDL cholesterol in the body (which doctors refer to as the "good" cholesterol) and an increase in highly sensitive C-reactive protein were predictors of a heart attack.

Here's how cholesterol works: Imagine your house is on fire. The fire department is called, and they rush to your house. The firemen attach their hoses to a fire hydrant and use water to put out the flames. In the body, inflammation is the fire, and cholesterol is the water coming out of the firemen's hose. The body lays down cholesterol in an effort to smother the inflammation. The end result is plaque buildup in the arteries — cholesterol that has gotten too thick and gummed up your arteries, reducing blood flow and increasing blood pressure, thereby increasing your risk of a heart attack and stroke.

Cholesterol is merely the body's strategy to deal with the inflammation. So is the cholesterol bad, or is the inflammation bad? Obviously, the inflammation is the culprit, and cholesterol is not only innocent — it's trying to help.

Cholesterol is produced naturally by the body, whether you choose to eat it or not. The body knows it needs cholesterol. Research in the *Journal of Atherosclerosis* showed that ten days after a person has a heart attack, cholesterol levels go up significantly. The researchers concluded that the increase in cholesterol is an effort to repair cells after the damage from a heart attack.

GEEK MOMENT: THE FRENCH PARADOX IS NOT A PARADOX!

The French are known to have low rates of heart disease, even though they eat high amounts of saturated fats. This is called "the French paradox." As you learned above, the idea of saturated fat being connected to heart disease is not a paradox at all.

French researchers compared margarine and butter. One group of subjects was fed margarine, and another group was fed butter. The margarine was made from safflower oil, a polyunsaturated fatty acid, supposedly a "healthier" fat.

Low-density lipoproteins (LDL) are known as "bad" cholesterol, whereas high-density lipoproteins (HDL) are considered "good" cholesterol. The margarine group lowered their LDL cholesterol eating margarine, but they also lowered their HDL cholesterol. The margarine hurt the bad guys, but it also hurt the good guys.

The authors concluded that butter was the better choice for heart health. But what's really interesting about this study is that the butter

group showed a significant rise in HDL cholesterol versus the margarine eaters. That means
eating butter raises your good cholesterol.

To further prove that the French paradox is not a
paradox, there's research showing that saturated
fats can actually protect the heart. Lipoprotein (a)
is considered an independent risk factor for heart
disease. It's even worse than LDL cholesterol.
The Diet and Human Performance laboratory in
Maryland performed research demonstrating that
subjects eating saturated fats lowered lipoprotein
(a) more than when eating oleic acid (the healthy
unsaturated fat in olive oil). In real-food terms, this
means that fats such as coconut oil and palm oil
can be heart-protective.

If you're a golfer over the age of forty, you should
have blood work done annually. Your cholesterol will be
checked to see if it is within a healthy range. If your cholesterol tests above 200 mg/dl, your doctor will probably recommend a cholesterol-lowering medication.

Always remember: you are responsible for your
health, and you always have a choice in whether or not
you take medication. Cholesterol is only one marker in
the blood that can indicate risk for heart disease. There
are other markers that are risk factors, such as:

- triglycerides
- highly sensitive C-reactive protein
- homocysteine
- high-density lipoproteins (HDL)
- lipoprotein (a)

GEEK MOMENT: CHOLESTEROL-LOWERING DRUGS

 Maybe you're taking a cholesterol-lowering medication or thinking about taking one because your doctor says your cholesterol is too high. Be wary of taking any drug. Statins are the top-selling drugs in the world. They lower cholesterol, but they will lower coenzyme Q10 (CoQ10) too. CoQ10 is very important for energy in the body. A common complaint among statin users is low energy. Another side effect is myopathy — muscle pain.

If you are on a statin and noticing side effects such as muscle pain that are not related to sports or exercise, consult with your physician. Consider supplementing with CoQ10 to replace what the drug is depleting.

If you are still on the fence about saturated fats and cholesterol, I would highly suggest reading the book *The Great Cholesterol Myth* by Stephen Sinatra, MD, and Jonny Bowden, PhD. This book goes into every detail of why saturated fats and cholesterol are not the problem when it comes to heart disease.

And Finally, the "Bad" Fat

So saturated fat and unsaturated fats are good. What, then, are the "bad" fats that everyone is worried about? Which ones are indisputably unhealthy for you?

The answer: trans fats.

As mentioned before, they're chemically altered. They're not natural. Examples are vegetable oils such as corn oil, cottonseed oil, and soybean oil, which are used to make margarine and appear in many of the baked goods, pastries, and snack foods you see in the grocery store.

All vegetable oils are very unstable because of the high amounts of omega-6 fatty acids in them. Heat causes instability. Therefore, if any vegetable oil is heated — i.e., you cook with it — the heating will convert the vegetable oil to trans fat.

According to fatty acid researcher Mary Enig, the average consumption of trans fatty acids has been reported to be 1.6 to 38.7 grams per person per day. The reason for the discrepancy is the variety of foods there are to eat. To limit your intake of trans fats, avoid the following foods:

Foods fried in vegetable oils

Any packaged food with partially hydrogenated oil

Junk foods (donuts, candy, and other stuff you know you have no business eating most of the time)

According to Sherry Rogers, MD, author of *Detoxify Or Die*, "When they replace the good oils in the cell membrane, hormone receptors no longer properly function and allergies surface. When trans fatty acids displace the good oils in the mitochondrial membrane inside the cell, they make it impossible to lose weight or to have boundless energy. They accelerate every disease and every facet of aging, making it impossible to completely heal any condition until the body's chemistry has been returned back to normal."

Some of the health problems that are associated with trans fats are:

• Lower HDL (good cholesterol)

- Increased LDL (bad cholesterol)
- Increased insulin levels
- Decreased testosterone levels
- Disrupted synthesis of essential fatty acids
- Increased number of fat cells

Even though you've probably been experiencing some of these health problems associated with trans fats, you can reverse them all. Choose to eat high-quality fats, and those fats will replace trans fats in your cells.

Monounsaturated Fats

We've established that, like saturated fats, monounsaturated fats are good. But I'll tell you a little more about them here. The best-known source of monounsaturated fat is olive oil. You may have heard of the benefits of olive oil from the famous Mediterranean Diet. People living in the Mediterranean region (Greece, Italy) have historically gotten most of their fatty acids from the consumption of olives and olive oil, and they have low rates of heart disease.

Olive oil contains oleic acid, which has been shown to decrease LDL cholesterol and triglycerides (fat in the bloodstream). Olive oil is rich in antioxidants and a substance called squalene, which has been shown to have anti-inflammatory properties and can slow blood-clot formation. It also enhances the absorption of omega-3 fatty acids within cells.

A lesser-known monounsaturated fat is palmitoleic acid. This is found mostly in macadamia nuts and in chicken fat. Macadamia nuts have the highest amount at over 20%. Palmitoleic acid has the added benefit of being antimicrobial. It helps to fight off bacteria and other pathogens.

Polyunsaturated Fats

You've heard me mention omega-3 fats several times now, and I know you've heard that they're healthy for you. This is the category they go under. The other well-known polyunsaturated acid is omega-6. Technically, polyunsaturated fats are referred to as linoleic acid (omega-6) and α-linolenic acid (omega-3). These fatty acids are considered essential. As with amino acids, "essential" means that the body can't make them, so we need to eat to obtain them.

Eating omega-6 and 3 fatty acids is important, but the ratio of the fatty acids is important as well. An imbalance of omega-6 to omega-3 fats can become a problem. Research by Artemis Simopoulos, MD, has shown that the average person's diet has twenty more times the omega-6 content than it does omega-3. Simopoulos says that the imbalanced ratio can lead to or exacerbate serious diseases such as:

- heart attack
- stroke
- cancer
- obesity
- insulin resistance
- diabetes
- asthma
- arthritis
- lupus
- depression
- schizophrenia
- attention deficit hyperactivity disorder (ADHD)
- postpartum depression
- Alzheimer's disease

For the record, an ideal balance of omega-6 to omega-3 fats is a ratio of 1:1. Most research indicates that we evolved on a diet that was 1:1. However, the Western diet has a skewed ratio that can be as high as 25:1. One of the main factors is the overconsumption of omega-6 fatty acids.

Many of the omega-6 fatty acids people consume come from too many vegetable oils in the diet and processed foods such as cereals and bread products. Reducing these types of foods will help balance out the omega-6 to 3 ratio. The problem with letting the ratio get out of whack is inflammation. Out-of-control inflammation can harm both a golfer's game and health. Examples would be joint aches and pains.

I consulted with a player that had constant low-back pain. Popping Advil before the round was routine for this player. But the pain became so intense that he had to start taking Vicodin — a very strong prescription painkiller — before he played. After analyzing the player's diet, I found that he was eating a massive amount of omega-6 fats and comparatively few omega-3s. After just a month spent eating an increased amount of omega-3 fats, the player's pain levels dropped by half!

Where Should We Get Fats?

I'm sure you've seen supplements like fish and krill oil, but you should always emphasize eating your fats from whole foods. Supplements can be helpful, but food is always preferable. One of the best sources of fat is red meat. Yes, you read it, red meat. Beef contains saturated fat, as well as unsaturated fat and some essential fatty acids. You get the deluxe package of fats when you eat red meat. You even get valuable vitamins such as vitamin D and B vitamins, along with minerals like zinc, selenium, and iron.

The Right Red Meat

There is one caveat about red meat. As with eggs and the chickens they came from, the fatty acids in red meat are dictated by what the cow ate. Therefore, it's important to eat red meat from grass-fed cows. California State University, Chico researcher Cynthia Daley performed a review of the fatty acid content and antioxidants in grain-fed beef versus grass-fed beef. Daley's work revealed major differences between grain-fed cows and grass-fed cows.

Grass-fed cows had:
- More omega-3 fats vs. omega-6
- More conjugated linoleic acid (CLA)
- More antioxidants (vitamins A, E, and superoxide dismutase)

Grass-fed cows have significantly more omega-3 fatty acids compared to grain-fed cows. Grain-fed cows have an overwhelming amount of omega-6 fatty acids. Consuming grain-fed meat further creates an omega-6 to 3 imbalance in your body. This is the main reason why there are so many studies showing that red meat causes a health risk. Studies about red meat and health typically use grain-fed red meat. It's not fair to judge grass-fed cows based on these results. A study must compare apples to apples and oranges to oranges. (Or, in this case, cows to cows.)

Conjugated linoleic acid (CLA) is referred to as alpha rumen acid because of its origin in the rumen of the cow. As a cow eats grass, the grass is digested and converted in the rumen to CLA. CLA has been shown to have anticancer properties. Dartmouth-Hitchcock Medical Center research has shown that CLA can inhibit the growth of cancer cells in women with stage I–III breast cancer. It's interesting to think that fighting cancer could be as simple as throwing a few hamburgers on the grill.

GEEK MOMENT: RED MEAT, THE NEW FAT-BURNER

 The Journal of International Medical Research gave a group of regular exercisers CLA and another group of exercisers a placebo. After twelve weeks, the CLA group lost a significant amount of body fat but no weight. Why didn't the scale go down? Because the CLA group gained muscle as well. Losing fat while gaining muscle at the same time is the Holy Grail for gym rats. You may not lose weight, but if you lose fat and put on muscle, you'll look better — and play better on the golf course.

If you've been told your whole life that red meat is bad for you because it causes everything from cancer to diabetes, I hope you'll finally consider adding it to your menu (or feel less guilty the next time you eat it).

Just remember that eating burgers from McDonald's isn't the same as a grass-fed steak from healthy cows.

Eggs

Whole eggs contain good amounts of cholesterol, saturated fat, monounsaturated fat, and omega-3 and 6 fatty acids. Choose pastured-range eggs to maximize the amount of omega-3 fat. Pasture-range eggs come from chickens that were allowed to forage outdoors and eat their natural diet. Like humans, chickens are omnivores, meaning they eat meat as well as plant foods. Chickens are meant to eat grasshoppers, worms, and other insects. Buying your eggs at a farmer's market raises your chances of finding an omega-3 rich dozen.

Artemis Simopoulos, author of *The Omega Diet*, analyzed eggs from pasture-range hens versus those raised in a feedlot (where most commercial chickens are kept). The pasture-range eggs had twenty times more omega-3's than the standard eggs. Furthermore, the ratio of omega-6 to omega-3 fats in the free-range eggs was 1:1. The control group eggs had a ratio of 20-to-1.

Butter

Butter has gotten the same bad rap as beef and eggs, but it's an excellent fat. It's very stable at high heat, so you can cook with it at fairly high temperature without it becoming unstable and turning dangerous.

If you can obtain butter from grass-fed cows, its fat will have high amounts of vitamin A as well as CLA. Butter is made up of short-chain fatty acids. Researchers at the University of Michigan have shown that short-chain fatty acids are antimicrobial, antifungal, and antiviral. This means that fats such as butter help our bodies fight bacteria and viruses.

Since butter is a short-chain fatty acid called butyric acid, it can be broken down easily for energy (short chains don't take long to break). Try cooking your eggs in butter in the morning, and you'll feel your energy levels take off.

Coconut Oil

For many years, movie theaters used coconut oil to pop their popcorn. When public fear of saturated fat became epidemic, they switched to vegetable oils. Recently, coconut oil has resurfaced, and rightly so. Since it's a saturated fat, coconut oil can be heated to high temperatures without it going rancid.

However, unlike butter, coconut oil is made up of medium-chain triglycerides (MCTs). These digest differently than any other type of saturated fat. They don't need to be digested in the stomach. Rather, they bypass the stomach and go directly to the liver, where they're immediately converted to energy. The great thing about MCTs is that they give you a similar burst of energy, like eating sugar does, but because it's a fat, it doesn't send your blood sugar on a roller coaster ride.

Coconut oil is made up of approximately 50% lauric acid. Bruce Fife, author of *The Coconut Oil Miracle*, says lauric acid is a potent antimicrobial fatty acid. Translation: it fights off the bad guys. So, if you want to prevent colds and flus, add coconut oil to your diet.

Acute and chronic inflammation is a major problem among golfers. Excess inflammation can exacerbate pain in an inflamed elbow or knee. Coconut oil has been shown to decrease inflammation. University of Southampton researchers performed studies on rats. They monitored their inflammation while feeding them different types of fats. For five weeks, the rats were fed olive oil, safflower oil, coconut oil, or fish oil. The rats fed coconut oil and fish oil showed significant decreases in inflammation markers (TNF alpha, IL-1B and IL-6). Not only did coconut oil show a decrease in inflammatory markers, but it also increased an anti-inflammatory cyctokine called IL-10. The moral of the story: eat coconut oil to help reduce inflammation in your body.

Studies performed by the College of Physicians and Surgeons show that MCTs have a significant impact on body weight. The researchers performed a study on thirty-one subjects for sixteen weeks, pitting MCT oil (similar to coconut oil) against olive oil. The subjects were randomly assigned to the MCT oil group or an olive oil (OO) group.

By the end of the study, all subjects that consumed MCT oil had lower body weights than the OO group. In addition, the members of the MCT group lost three times the fat that the OO group did.

For these reasons, I recommend eating coconut products whenever you can — provided, of course, that they're from whole, natural sources. Cook your food in coconut oil. When you're in a rush, eat food bars that contain coconut. And instead of dairy, drink coconut milk.

Are you still thinking that fat is bad for the heart?

I'll use one more piece of evidence to make my case. Another study by researcher Marie-Pierre St-Onge evaluated the effects of MCTs on heart-disease risk factors. Subjects were fed MCTs for a sixteen-week weight-loss program, and metabolic syndrome markers (which indicate heart-disease risk) were monitored. The conclusion: MCT oil consumption "does not have detrimental effects on cardiovascular disease risk factors."

Blood-Sugar Control

It's been a long time since the beginning of this chapter (you're doing great, by the way!). If you'll recall, I said the main reason I love fat is it helps prevent blood-sugar spikes. Remember the goal is always to flatline your blood sugar. This creates an environment for stable and long-lasting energy.

University of Toronto researchers studied the effects of macronutrients on blood sugar. They tested the effects of carbohydrates, proteins, and fats on blood sugar. They fed subjects an equal amount of calories in the form of all three nutrients. When fat and protein were eaten, there was virtually no rise in blood sugar. When subjects ate carbs, there was a rise in blood glucose and then a quick dropoff. The dreaded blood sugar roller coaster!

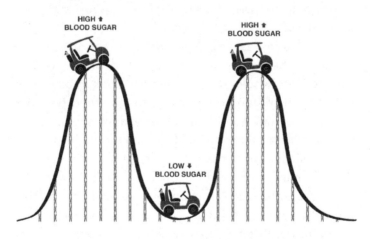

As you can see, it pays to focus on fat and protein in your diet. This avoids the sharp blood sugar ups and downs you get with only carb consumption. But, as many nutritionists say, athletes need carbs — and lots of them — because they're the body's main source of energy during exercise.

This is 100% true ... but only partially.

A typical scenario is an athlete who wakes up early

to eat breakfast. The player's hope is to get energy for competition later that day. Most will grab a bowl of cereal with nonfat milk. But this has disastrous consequences on performance.

The cereal digests almost as fast as sugar itself. Secondly, because there's no fat in the milk, there's nothing to slow down the digestive process. In addition, the lactose (another sugar) in milk will add to the blood sugar spike. This makes the blood sugar roller coaster worse.

Initially, this player may feel full of energy, but as blood sugar crashes, energy will go down. Symptoms such as irritability and a lack of focus will appear. Hunger is another problem. A golfer will be hungry within an hour or two because the food digests so rapidly.

Golf is a unique sport that takes four to five hours to play. Maintaining energy levels and minimizing hunger over this time is key to helping a player focus the entire round. This is where fat really comes into play. Fat has virtually no impact on blood sugar, and eating fat will help to satiate an athlete. This prevents the player from being preoccupied with hunger, and they can focus on the game at hand.

9
THE
FUNDAMENTALS
OF FIBER

Fiber is the third component of the PFF system I've been describing. Most people think of fiber as a tool to keep you "regular," but it offers a lot more than just protection from constipation.

Fiber has been shown to bind to toxins in our body, lower cholesterol, slow glucose absorption, improve insulin sensitivity, lower blood pressure, aid in weight loss, lessen free radical damage from fats, and have anti-inflammatory properties.

Fiber comes in two categories: insoluble and soluble. The insoluble kind is the one that helps you poop. It can't be digested in the body, so it passes through it. Think of insoluble fiber as a broom for your intestines. It clears out any gunk (foods that haven't digested) from your digestive system. Soluble fiber, on the other hand, supports the good bacteria in your gut.

At any given time we have approximately three to four pounds of bacteria in our intestinal tract. (A yucky thought, I know.) We are all walking balls of bacteria! But there's good bacteria and bad bacteria. In order for us to be healthy, there must be a delicate balance of the two. When the bad guys are outnumbering the good guys, you'll get symptoms such as constipation, diarrhea, bloating, gas, farts, belching, and even acid reflux. Soluble fiber supplies the army of good bacteria. They feed on it. The more fiber you eat, the more the good guys grow and support your digestive system.

Besides the benefit of gut function, both types of fiber help with blood sugar control. Whenever fiber is eaten, it slows down the absorption of blood sugar. When fiber is added to a mix of proteins, fats, and other carbohydrates, it forms a thick, viscous mixture. This mixture is slowly broken down and released into the bloodstream. This flatlines blood sugar, preventing the blood sugar roller coaster.

What's the Best Fiber?

To you, fiber might conjure up one word: Metamucil. However, drinking some lab-made orange concoction isn't the way you were supposed to consume fiber. Fiber exists in abundance in whole foods, and that's how you should be getting it. In fact, whole foods tend to offer a two-for-one deal: both insoluble and soluble fiber in one shot. Metamucil powders only contain insoluble fiber.

The best source of fiber is vegetables. Not only are they loaded with fiber, but they also pack many other nutrients your body needs: vitamins, minerals, and phytonutrients.

Notice that I mentioned vegetables rather than fruits. In my experience, most people think vegetables and fruit are the same. They offer similar benefits, but fruits have significant amounts of sugar, while most veggies are low in sugar.

Fruit is easier to overeat than vegetables. Since people enjoy the taste, they tend to eat much more than a serving. Until my intervention, I found some of my athletes would eat half a watermelon in one sitting! You just don't hear of that happening with a similar amount of broccoli. A single serving of fruit (one piece, or a cup full/the size of your fist) usually doesn't pack much sugar. Huge amounts of fruit cause a burst in blood sugar then a quick drop off. Keep this in mind when you're eating fruit, and fill up on more vegetables instead.

GEEK MOMENT: IS EATING ORGANIC WORTH IT?

 In the past two decades, controversy about the safety and nutritional quality of our food — particularly produce — has become big news. One camp says to eat USDA-certified organic food, while others say that conventionally raised (and much less expensive) fruits and vegetables are just as good.

Due to nutrient loss in soil, my take is that non-organic foods have fewer vitamins and minerals than organic fruits and veggies. Science backs me up on this.

Researcher Virginia Worthington, M.S., has shown that organic vegetables have more nutrients than their conventionally grown counterparts. The following is a table adapted from her review of the most commonly studied vegetables and the mean difference of organic vegetables versus conventional as the baseline. You can see that by far, organic foods have more nutrients than conventional vegetables (in most cases, although not all). In the long run, you get what you pay for.

Vegetable	Vitamin C	Iron	Magnesium	Phosphorus
Lettuce	+17%	+17%	+29%	+14%
Spinach	+52%	+25%	-13%	+14%
Carrot	-6%	+12%	+69%	+13%
Potato	+22%	+21%	+5%	0%
Cabbage	+43%	+41%	+40%	+22%

What About Grains?

Grains are often recommended for their fiber content, so people shove down cereal, bread, and pasta without a second thought. These foods do contain fiber, but remember, they're processed. Before this food gets to your plate, the grain it came from has been ground, heated, pressurized, and processed. It contains very little nutritional value.

I believe there is an overprescription of carbs among athletes today. I'm not against eating carbs by any means, but I am against eating the wrong type and eating carbs at the wrong time. The following carbs must be kept to a minimum:
- cereals
- toast/bread
- bagels
- pasta

It's really easy to overeat these foods. These are the ones that really elevate blood sugar. Think about every Italian dinner you've had. How did you feel when you left the table? It's easy to get bloated on bread and pasta, but have you ever pushed away from a dinner table saying, "Boy, I ate way too much spinach tonight?" It never happens.

Just as there is a different golf club for every shot, different circumstances call for different carbs. It's all about timing. Vegetables can be eaten all the time because of their fiber content and richness of nutrients, but grains ... not so much.

Why Do I Need Carbs At All?

Carbs are the primary fuel used during exercise, so it's important to have carbs in and around exercise. But too much of a good thing can be detrimental.

First, forget what you've heard about "carb-loading" with plates of pasta, bowls of cereal, and loaves of bread. This was a strategy used by marathon runners and other endurance athletes who need to perform at a steady rate for long periods, This practice has fallen out of favor even with them in recent years.

Overeating carbs leads to three problems. One, it displaces the other macronutrients your body needs — protein and fats. Two, excess carbs create the roller coaster effect on blood sugar. Lastly, excess carbs can actually deplete your vitamins and minerals.

As mentioned earlier, excess carbs elevate blood sugar. The body's response is to release insulin to manage the blood sugar. Elevated insulin levels are fine for short periods of time, but chronically elevated insulin levels due to excess carb consumption deplete vitamins and minerals. Magnesium is a mineral that is vital for health and performance. (More on this magnificent mineral later in the supplement chapter). University of Naples researchers have shown the elevated levels of insulin increase losses of magnesium in urine. In addition, the Vitamin and Mineral Laboratory of the US Department of Agriculture has shown elevated insulin depletes chromium. Chromium is a trace mineral that is important for blood sugar control. Research confirms this type of depletion of key nutrients, as well as my observations with organic acid testing (urine).

There are several reasons why carbs are overeaten. But mainly, they're just awfully convenient. Carbs are easy to prepare and cost less than protein. They're quick to eat (a bowl of cereal goes down faster than a plate of eggs and vegetables), and they taste great.

But don't worry. You won't sacrifice flavor on my program. You'll learn ways to make protein and fat taste more delicious than any pasta, cereal, or bread you ever tasted.

Types of Carbs

There are two different densities of carbs. The first is what I refer to as glucose density. This is a type of carb that has a high amount of starch that turns into glucose in your bloodstream. A potato would be considered a high-density glucose (HDG) carb. The second type of density is what I refer to as nutrient density. This is a carb that has a high amount of fiber, vitamins, minerals, and phytonutrients. Spinach would be considered a high-density nutrient (HDN) carb.

Vegetables are number one on the list when it comes to carb intake, because it is a HDN carb. As we've discussed, vegetables contain key vitamins and minerals. For example, spinach is one of the best ways to increase your calcium intake. One cup of spinach contains 240 milligrams of calcium, which is almost the same amount as in a cup of milk. Second, vegetables offer fiber, which helps flatline your blood sugar. Third, veggies contain phytonutrients that make you healthier. These include antioxidants that help fight the damage you create from daily workouts in the gym and rounds on the course.

GEEK MOMENT: THE MOST IMPORTANT VEGGIE

 I'm often asked, "Rob, if you could only eat one vegetable the rest of your life, what would it be?" I say broccoli, hands down. I choose broccoli because it has a special phytochemical called diindolylmethane (DIM).

Research by Michael A. Zeligs in the Journal of Medicinal Food has shown that DIM is the kick-starter for key enzymes called P450 isozymes. These isoenzymes are critical for the metabolism of estrogens, the feminine hormone.

Estrogens are naturally produced in the bodies of both males and females. Obviously, females produce more than males. The problem these days is the prevalence of estrogen mimickers — chemicals that function like estrogen in the body but are not produced by it naturally.

The most prevalent estrogen mimicker is bisphenol A (BPA), the chemical I warned you about in plastic water bottles. It was developed as a synthetic estrogen in the 1890s. BPA is found in feeding bottles and the internal coating of cans. The scary truth is BPA is released into water and food.

Researchers of the Journal of Medicinal Food showed that 90% of the BPA people encounter is from their food, and most people have detectable amounts of BPA in their urine. When your body is bombarded by estrogen like this, it raises your risk for diseases like cancer and will greatly slow down the results you want to see in the gym or on the course.

Therefore, I believe it's really critical to eat a cruciferous vegetable on a daily basis for its DIM. These include:

- arugula
- bok choy
- broccoli
- brussels sprouts
- cabbage
- cauliflower
- collard greens
- daikon
- kale
- radish
- turnips
- watercress

In addition to DIM, cruciferous vegetables contain high amounts of sulphur, which is the element that accounts for the stinky smell of broccoli. Put up with the smell, because sulphur helps to activate the most powerful antioxidant in your body. Richard Lord, author of *Laboratory Evaluations for Integrative and Functional Medicine*, states that cruciferous vegetables up-regulate an antioxidant called glutathione S-transferase. Glutathione S-transferase is a compound that is found in every cell of your body. Not only does glutathione detox your body of chemicals, it's also profoundly important for the immune system. German researchers have shown the lymphoid cells of the immune system are dependent on adequate levels of glutathione.

Fruits are number two on the list. As mentioned earlier, they have many of the same benefits as vegetables but contain sugar. When a golfer is experiencing a blood sugar roller coaster due to fruit consumption, the solution is usually twofold. One, cut back on the amount of fruit being eaten in a sitting, and two, combine it with some protein and fat to slow down its digestion.

As with any food, it's easy to fall into a pattern of eating the most convenient fruits or our very favorite ones. Step out of your comfort zone and try other fruits. For instance, berries have higher amounts of antioxidants than tropical fruits. However, pineapple contains enzymes that help digest food and reduce inflammation. Eat a variety of fruits to get the best of both worlds.

GEEK MOMENT: GOLFERS DON'T NEED CARBS LIKE "ATHLETES" DO

 The reason carbs are overemphasized in the diets of athletes is the use of research based on endurance athletes. Runners, cyclists, and swimmers are athletes who burn tremendous calories in their training and competition. They have extreme energy needs. As a result, they need more carbohydrates than any other athletes.

Research by Michael Gleeson of the University of Birmingham indicates that athletes involved in "heavy training" should consume carbs as 60% of their diet. This breaks down to 8 to 10 grams of carbs per kilogram of body weight. Those carbs are used to restore liver and muscle glycogen, the stored form of carbohydrate in the body, which provides energy during activity.

Let's say you're 150 pounds. There are 2.2 kilograms in a pound, so you'd weigh 68 kilos. Multiply that by ten and that's 680 grams of carbs you need per day.

What does 680 grams of carbs look like? Well, one cup of rice is about 50 grams of carbs. To eat this recommended amount of carbs in rice, you'd need to choke down thirty cups per day.

Mmm, sounds delicious, eh?

Before you start trying to eat buckets of rice, you have to ask some questions. What exactly is "heavy training"? Gleeson refers to heavy training as exercise performed for more than two hours per day. But then what kind of exercise are we talking about?

The only athletes who train for two hours daily are endurance athletes. Marathon runners, cyclists, and triathletes perform continuous exercise — no stopping — for that length of time. Of course this kind of activity will require more carbs than other sports.

Most sports do not require anywhere near the level of endurance. The top five sports played in the world are: football (soccer), field hockey, cricket, tennis, and volleyball. These sports are NOT pure endurance sports. They're "stop-and-go" sports. There are periods of movement followed by rest. In addition, their games/events are not as long as those of endurance sports. Therefore, the need for carbs among athletes who play them is much less. Golfers don't need a ton of carbs for long-lasting energy. If you eat carbs according to the needs of an endurance athlete, you'll only send your blood sugar skyrocketing and end up fatter.

The Window of Opportunity

When you're exercising, muscles are contracting. You're sweating, huffing, and puffing, muscles are being broken down, energy sources are being used, and hormones are beginning to fluctuate. This is a stress on your body, and it will require nutrients as soon as you're done in order to begin the recovery process.

When you're performing exercises such as squats, pushups, or lunges, muscle tissue is being broken down on a microscopic level. This is called protein breakdown. That's okay in the short term, but you want to stimulate muscle protein synthesis (MPS) after a workout. This is critical so muscles can repair and build back bigger and stronger. The sooner you can turn on the MPS switch, the faster you'll recover.

There are several factors when it comes to a faster recovery time. Timing of the meal after training can have significant affects on recovery, as well as the composition of the post-workout meal. Studies show that you can make this reversal rapidly.

Timing of Nutrients

Timing of nutrients is really important to turn on protein synthesis. Vanderbilt University Medical Center had subjects exercise moderately for sixty minutes. After the exercise session, they immediately gave one group a drink composed of protein, carbohydrates, and fat. A second group received the same drink three hours later.

The subjects who imbibed right away showed a THREEFOLD increase in protein synthesis versus the subjects who had to wait to drink. There was also a net increase in leg protein synthesis with the first group, while the second group showed a net loss of leg protein because of the delay.

Think of your muscles as a sponge. Before you exercise, they're full of carbs, similar to a sponge full of water. During exercise, the glycogen (carbs) in muscles becomes wrung out, like a sponge can have water squeezed out of it. At the end of the training session, your muscles are depleted of carbs (The degree of depletion depends on the intensity of the workout). Similar to a dry sponge, muscles are ready to soak up any carbs you consume, along with amino acids to help rebuild muscle protein and other nutrients.

There's only one catch: you have a limited amount of time to take advantage of this condition. After you finish your last set, the window slowly begins to close. University of Texas researchers have demonstrated delaying the consumption of carbohydrates by two hours dramatically decreased the repletion of glycogen in the muscles.

GEEK MOMENT: DON'T FORGET THE PROTEIN?

 Since muscles are made up of protein, it only makes sense to eat protein after a workout. There's a ton of research to confirm the importance of protein postworkout.

Journal of Metabolism researchers put subjects through a fourteen-week resistance training program. They were given an isocaloric protein (25 grams) or carbohydrate (25 grams) supplement before and immediately after training sessions. Their results showed the protein group increased growth of type I and type II muscle fibers, whereas there were no changes in the carbohydrate group. In addition to the increase in muscle, there were improvements in squat jump height in the protein group, but not in the carbohydrate group. The carbohydrate group did show in an increase in countermovement jump and strength.

The significance of this study is to point to the importance of protein postworkout. Does that mean that carbs have no benefit? Absolutely not! As mentioned above, carbs replete glycogen and taking in carbs and protein give a synergistic effect on recovery.

Think of it as: 1+1= 3 effect.

University of Western Ontario researchers have shown liquid carbohydrate + protein was much more efficient than carbohydrate alone in the repletion of glycogen.

You're Not Too Old to Put on Muscle!

I know what you're thinking: "I'm too old to build muscle." I've got news for you: you can! The Sports Medicine Research Unit in Denmark put elderly males of the average age of seventy-four on a twelve-week resistance training program. The subjects were separated into two groups. The first group was given a postworkout drink (10 grams protein, 7 grams carbohydrates, 3 grams fat) immediately after each exercise session, whereas the second group was given the drink two hours after the exercise session. Biopsies of the quadriceps muscle showed a significant area of growth, whereas the second group showed no changes. It doesn't matter your age when it comes to postworkout nutrition, but the timing does matter. Make sure you have a postworkout drink to maximize muscle and recovery.

GEEK MOMENT: WHEN YOU WORK OUT, YOU BECOME HORMONAL — IN A GOOD WAY!

 Anabolic (tissue-building) hormones such as testosterone (T) are produced during weight-training sessions. The more T you produce during a session, the faster you'll recover from it. That is, if you can manage to keep cortisol in check at the same time.

As I wrote earlier, cortisol (C) is the antithesis of testosterone. It's a stress hormone released in response to the stress of exercise. So, although your body is producing an anabolic hormone, it's producing a catabolic one too. There's a see-saw battle going on.

Finnish researchers have determined the higher the ratio of testosterone to cortisol (T:C), the faster you recover from exercise. The goal is to maintain the peak level of T and decrease C after a workout. The net effect is a state of anabolism. Research by William Kraemer of Pennsylvania State University has shown that a postworkout drink immediately after exercise rapidly decreases C.

The biggest benefit that I've seen is less soreness. Whether you're a touring professional or a week-end golfer, soreness can derail your golf game. A common routine with older golfers is to pop a few Advil before a round to "take the edge off." The soreness that occurs in muscles is a sign of incomplete recovery. Once I have these players eat the right food after a round, the soreness is no longer there.

As you probably guessed, a five-minute workout doesn't give you a license to pig out. The carbs you eat should be proportionate to your size and the intensity of your training. If you train forty-five to sixty minutes in the gym, use the chart at the bottom of page as a guideline for the amount of protein and carbs you should take in after training. Generally speaking, your carb intake at this time should be twice your protein intake.

Bodyweight (lbs.)	Protein Intake	Carbohydrate Intake
125	20 g (1 serving of protein or 1 scoop whey protein	40g (1 cup of starch or 1 cup of fruit with whey protein)
175	30 g (1 serving of protein or 1.5 scoop whey protein	60g (1.5 cups of starch or 1.5 cups of fruit with whey protein)
>200	40 g (1 serving of protein or 2 scoop whey protein	80g (2 cups of starch or 2 cups of fruit with whey protein)

* size of a deck of cards for protein   * size of fist for starch

What About After Golf?

Golf counts as exercise, but it's not on the same level of intensity as a resistance workout. You tear down muscle, but to a lesser degree. In general, I recommend reducing the amount of carbs you'd ingest after a workout by half when you're just finishing up a round of golf. So if you'd normally consume 40 grams of carbs after lifting weights, have about 20 grams. This could be in the form of a light meal or whey protein powder with a banana. If time is of the essence, go for the whey protein powder. If you've got time to sit down for lunch with your golf buddies, have a meal that consists of lean protein, a bit of starch, and veggies.

However, body composition is a factor to consider too. If you're overweight and want to lose fat, just eat protein and veggies after a round of golf. You don't need more carbs when you're already having trouble processing them. However, if you're a lean, lanky junior that needs to gain weight, feel free to double your carb intake.

GEEK MOMENT: "CARBS GO RIGHT TO MY MUSCLES!"

The Journal of Sports Medicine has shown that carbs are depleted in the Type IIb fibers of strength and power athletes (golfers fall into this category). Type IIb fibers are the muscle fibers that are responsible for running fast, jumping high, and hitting a long drive. Therefore, it's important to get carbs into these muscle fibers so that they can recover and perform optimally. Be sure to have carbs as soon as you finish your round.

Watch the Clock

Timing is really important with this meal. All the studies mentioned previously had one thing in common: they showed that the earlier subjects took in carbs and protein the better.

After you finish your last rep in the gym, the timer starts and the window slowly begins to close. Eat something as soon as possible within an hour of finishing exercise or a round of golf.

What Should I Eat?

I've been telling you to reduce high-density glucose (HDG) carbs throughout the day, but after exercise is the perfect time to eat them. These types of HDG carbs will rapidly elevate blood sugar, which is exactly what you want postexercise. Elevating blood sugar requires the production of insulin, the hormone that helps to shuttle glucose and amino acids into muscle cells. The faster the carbs get into the blood, the faster they enter your muscles. This is the time to eat carbs such as rice, potatoes, quinoa, sweet potatoes, and oats. Fruits such as pineapple, mango, and papaya are great choices too. There's no need to break out a food scale. On average, a cup of starch is about 40 grams of HDG carbs. The size of a closed fist is almost equivalent to a cup.

Don't forget to eat lean protein sources too. Lean meats such as chicken, turkey, eggs, and lean cuts of red meat will help stop the catabolism of muscles and start that rebuilding process. A serving of protein about the size of a deck of cards provides 20 grams. If you weigh 125 pounds, you should eat a deck's worth of protein. Add another deck every 50 pounds you weigh over that. I've touted whole foods this entire section, but sometimes supplementation may be more optimal after a workout.

GEEK MOMENT: THE POSTWORKOUT SHAKE (PWS)

 Whole foods are always the priority, but postworkout is a special situation where supplementation can be more effective. All the studies I mentioned used proteins and carbs in a liquid state. Whole foods take time to digest, and most studies agree that liquid form is the fastest method for absorption. Timing is of critical importance, so having nutrients that are readily available speeds up recovery. This is where protein powders can really be of benefit.

The most commonly used protein powder is whey protein. Many people use whey protein because of the high amount of branched-chain amino acids (BCAAs) it provides. BCAAs are made up of three amino acids called leucine, isoleucine, and valine. They are responsible for increasing protein synthesis, among other things. For this reason, many people use whey protein daily after exercise. Whey is a great protein source, but I've found some golfers and athletes just can't tolerate it. Symptoms such as congestion, bloating, and gas after drinking a shake are signs your body is not digesting the whey properly.

If you're a person that's been using whey protein daily and have been reactive, don't worry. You can get all the same benefits of whey as you can with other proteins. Research in the Journal of Strength and Conditioning took forty-one females and males and had subjects drink a PWS that consisted of beef protein isolate, hydro-lyzed chicken protein, or whey protein isolate. All groups showed a significant gain in muscle mass and loss of fat mass during the eight-week study.

Sometimes it's good to give the body a break. There are many other types of protein powders on the market. There's rice, pea, egg, and even beef protein. I like to rotate protein powders each day to avoid an intolerance. See the chart below for a sample schedule. You can start with whey on Day One, then cycle through all the other powders and go back to it and repeat the cycle.

Day 1	Day 2	Day 3	Day 4
Whey	Egg	Beef	Plant-based

Now that you've got your protein source set, let's talk about the carbs. Since you'll be mixing protein and carbs together, there's no need to add tons of carbs. Research in the *American Journal of Clinical Nutrition* has shown that a mixture of protein and carbs gets the job done just as well as a high amount of carbs.

I instruct all my players to premake their PWS before heading to the gym. The second they finish their last rep, they walk to their PWS shake and start drinking it. This is the most efficient way to take advantage of the postworkout window.

There's no "magic ingredient" that will make you perform on the course, but controlling your blood sugar can lead to some miraculous improvements. Following the PFF formula makes it possible.

10
FAQS ABOUT WHOLE FOODS

A few buddies of mine follow a plan that has them skip breakfast. They said it's called Intermittent Fasting (IF). Is this something I should follow?

I first learned about IF from a colleague of mine, John Berardi (JB). We were presenting at the same conference, and after we finished our presentations, we went to the gym for a workout. As we were working out, we were "geeking out" on nutrition. As I finished my set, John told me he was fasting. I thought he meant he was fasting on a short-term basis for detox purposes. But he said he was fasting on a daily basis. That caught my attention because JB was a big proponent of five to six meals per day. He told me he was fasting all through the morning then started eating at noon and ended with dinner. He looked lean and healthy. It piqued my interest, so I decided to experiment with IF. That was back in 2010.

The basis of IF is a window of fasting followed by a refeed window. For example, a common protocol is the

16/8. Fast for sixteen hours then refeed for eight hours. So, you would finish dinner by 8:00 p.m. then fast through the morning and begin the refeed period at noon.

Intermittent fasting is not new. It's been around for some time. It can be very successful for some people, but when it comes to golfers, I would advise against the use of it for several reasons. First, blood sugar control is of utmost importance for stable energy. IF advocates skipping breakfast and eating lunch as the first meal. Most golfers tee off in the morning. Imagine not eating breakfast and trying to concentrate during an entire round of golf! I've found a player is focused on food rather than golf!

Second, since blood sugar will be lower than normal, mood can be greatly affected. Think of a child that hasn't eaten lunch or a snack. Probably whiny, crying and a handful to deal with. In the same way, a player could be irritable and moody when trying to implement IF. Instead of being in control of your emotions, the lack of blood sugar can create an environment that creates unstable emotions, leading to irrational decisions on the course.

Experimenting with IF can be disastrous if you don't have good eating habits. Since you skip breakfast and don't eat anything all morning, you'll be very hungry once lunch comes around. Most players don't have good eating habits, so therefore when they break the fast and "refeed," they tend to go on the "see-food" diet, eating everything in sight! If you're one of those players that has great solid eating habits and want to do a little self-experimentation, go ahead and give IF a try. Go ahead and download JB's free e-book, *Experimenting with Intermittent Fasting*.

I'm just not hungry in the morning, so it's really difficult to eat breakfast. What can I do to increase my appetite in the morning?

If you're the type of golfer who eats like a king at night, then you're going to have no appetite in the morning. Simply put, you're back-loading most of your calories at night, so it makes sense that you're not going have an appetite in the morning. The reason you're eating like a king at night is because you need to. If you don't eat enough calories throughout the day, you're going to overeat at night. Part of the solution is to eat breakfast. Even if you don't have an appetite in the morning, eat something small. It could be a hardboiled egg or a few turkey slices. Gradually build this up over time. This will help control appetite for lunch and later in the evening. You'll begin to notice you won't be as ravenous at night.

Can't I just drink a smoothie for breakfast before the round?

You can drink a smoothie for breakfast, but it's not the best option, especially before golf. There are several reasons why it's not the best option. First, smoothies are in a liquid state, so digestion is a lot faster. This causes blood sugar to go up faster than with a whole food meal. This would be ideal after golf, but not before. Second, most smoothies are carb-dominant. Since smoothies are full of fruit, fruit juice, and even sorbet, this blows up the sugar content, leading to the blood sugar roller coaster. Third, there's barely any protein or fat in the smoothie, so hunger hits you a lot faster during the round. As I said before, it's not the best option, but if you're going to make a smoothie, make sure you maximize nutrition and PFF (protein, fat, fiber). The base should always be some kind of protein powder. Use a liquid such as coconut milk that has some fats, as well as a fat source such as almond butter or seeds such as chia seeds. Use fruit such as berries for increased fiber intake. You'll find a recipe under 10 Quick Breakfast Options that uses the PFF principle.

My friend told me there was a study that showed that protein causes cancer. Should I be concerned about eating more protein?

The study you're referring to is the book *The China Study* by T. Colin Campbell. I was constantly asked about my opinion of this book when it was first published. I eventually got around to reading it so I could be familiar with Campbell's ideas about nutrition. When I came to the part about protein and cancer, I was very intrigued. He referred to a study that showed a high-protein animal-based diet increased cancer growth. I was actually a bit worried and possibly thought animal-based protein diets may not be so good after all. That was until I investigated Campbell's sources.

Campbell was referencing a study with rats fed a high-protein animal diet. Rats induced with cancer were fed a 20% protein diet, and another group were fed a 5% protein diet. The results of the study showed a growth of cancer cells in the 20% protein group, whereas the 5% protein group didn't show growth of cancer cells. If you're a layperson, it's quite alarming news; however, if you're a trained scientific professional, there's more to the story. Campbell's "proof" of high protein causing cancer growth is bad science at best. The big issue with this "proof" is the use of rats as subjects. In research, animal studies are considered preliminary studies to confirm a hypothesis. At this point, further studies should be performed on humans to confirm this finding. Campbell jumped the gun by using this sort of study to fit into his hypothesis. The last time I looked in the mirror, I wasn't a rat, and neither are you!

The other big issue with Campbell's "proof" is his assertion that the type of protein is important in the context of cancer growth. In fact, in his book he has a section titled "All Proteins Are Not Alike."

In addition to the quantity of protein, animal protein was shown to increase cancer growth, whereas plant protein at the same levels does not cause cancer growth. Campbell took this information, ran with it, and assumed that all animal proteins cause cancer. The animal protein that was fed to the rats was casein. Casein is the main protein found in dairy. Rats (wild rats) are omnivores that eat mostly grains, fruits, vegetables, seeds, and nuts, as well as bugs and other small animals. Rats don't drink milk!

Of all the animal proteins, casein is the most allergenic type of protein that you can consume. I have performed many food sensitivity tests on players. Casein (i.e., dairy) is the most common food that people react to. Reactions can manifest as stuffy nose, mucous buildup, as well as skin conditions such as eczema and acne. Not to mention gas, bloating, and diarrhea.

It makes perfect sense the rats fed casein had higher rates of cancer, since rats don't eat casein as a protein source. For Campbell to extrapolate and say that all animal protein causes cancer is horrible science. He should know better than that, being a "scientist." In review, avoid dairy but eat your chicken, beef, fish, and eggs. You'll thank me for it. If you want further information about protein intake, read the following protein debate between Loren Cordaine, PhD and T. Colin Campbell, PhD.

www.catalystathletics.com/articles/downloads/proteinDebate.pdf

You've mentioned grass-fed red meat several times. Is organic red meat the same thing?

Grass-fed red meat (i.e., pasture-fed) and organic red meat are two completely different types of meat. In the United States, there's a difference between the two types of meats. However, in some countries, there's only one type of red meat. Several years ago, I spoke on nutrition at the Colombia Federation for Golf. I was discussing the importance of eating grass-fed red meat versus grain-fed red meat. But I began to see confused faces. I talked to the translator, and he told me there's no grain-fed meat in Colombia. Cattle ranchers simply allow cattle to do what they do: eat grass!

Feeding cows grain is a practice used in the United States to fatten up the animals rapidly but at a cost. This practice in the cattle industry creates a vicious cycle. Since cows are unable to digest grains, they become sick. Sick cows can't be sold, so they feed them antibiotics. And it goes on and on. As a result of cows eating grains, this changes the meat drastically. The grain consumption leads to high amounts of omega-6 fatty acids in the red meat. This leads to imbalances of fatty acids in the body and contributes to inflammation. Be aware when you shop for red meat. When a steak is labeled "organic," it simply means that the cows were fed "organic" grains. It still makes the cows sick and is loaded with too many omega-6 fatty acids. Whenever possible, purchase "grass-fed" or "pasture-fed" red meat.

What type of fat should I add to my meals?

It's good to add a variety of fats to your meals. Avocado, nuts, and seeds are great types of fats that can be added as a side to the meal. Adding cooking oils such as butter, coconut oil, palm oil, and olive oil can increase fat in a meal. Start with one tablespoon of fat first and assess how you feel. If you feel good during a round of golf, then don't add more. If you have the "more is better" attitude, you may overdo it. The classic sign that you overdid it is nausea or diarrhea.

What about chocolate milk after a workout?

This is a popular recommendation for recovery, but I have several issues with chocolate milk. It's based on research that the optimal ratio of carbohydrate to protein is 4 to 1 for glycogen repletion. One cup of chocolate milk has carbohydrates and protein that is close to this ratio. Remember that glycogen (stored form of carbs in muscle) becomes depleted from exercise, and glycogen repletion is important for muscle recovery. However, it depends on the type and duration of exercise performed that impacts glycogen depletion. As mentioned earlier, most of these studies are done with endurance athletes who exercise for hours at a time and multiple sessions per day. In this case, yes, the high amount of carbs would be necessary for repletion of muscles of this type of athlete. Golf is a sport that doesn't deplete massive amounts of carbohydrate. Even if you performed a high-intensity workout for forty-five minutes, carb depletion is moderate. Therefore, a 4 to 1 ratio of carbs to protein is too many carbs, which will make you fat!

Besides the high carb intake, I don't like the type of protein in chocolate milk. Casein is the main type of protein found in chocolate milk. It's the most allergenic type of protein that you can consume. This is a big concern of mine, because it's the recommendation for many of our young junior players. It's recommended because it's convenient, but there are side effects that many players experience.

Symptoms include:

- runny nose
- constant clearing of the throat
- skin conditions (eczema, hives, rashes)
- diarrhea
- constipation
- bloating and gas
- dark circles under eyes

If you have any of these symptoms, try avoiding chocolate milk and any other dairy products for a month, and you may notice many of these symptoms will disappear.

Another reason to avoid chocolate milk is the amount of sugar. We all know sugar is not good for you, but in the context of the postworkout window, it's the worst thing to consume. After workouts, the immune system is slightly depressed, so it's therefore important to upregulate the immune system. However, sugar has been shown to depress the immune system. Think of the immune system as Pac-Man. In the same way that Pac-Man eats ghosts, phagocytes eat up invaders to prevent attacks on the immune system. This is called the phagocytic index (the number of invaders eaten by phagocytes). When sugar is eaten, the phagocytic index is lowest two hours after eating sugar. So, when your body should be protecting itself and repairing, it can't.

Are there any postworkout smoothie recipes that you recommend?

What's important about the smoothie recipe is it has high-quality proteins, carbs, and tastes good! Here's a template of what it should consist of:

- 1/2 cup organic juice (pineapple, cherry, apricot, grape)
- 1/2 cup cold water
- 1 cup of organic frozen berries
- 1 scoop of protein powder (beef, chicken, egg, pea, rice, whey)

This template gives you about a 1:1 ratio of protein and carbohydrates. The juices add in glucose that will raise blood sugar to help shuttle in carbs and protein into muscles. The frozen berries add in antioxidants to help prevent the pinball effect of exercise. Try different combinations and see what you like best.

I play early in the winter, and I'm freezing. I try to drink coffee or tea, but it makes me feel wired. Is there anything warm I can drink during a round?

A great hot drink to consume is bone broth. Bone broth is very popular these days. It's touted to benefit healing of the GI tract and for joint health. It has high amounts of an amino acid called glycine. Glycine is the amino acid that's imperative for the reconstruction of joints. Heat up a cup or two and add unrefined sea salt to taste. It's great to keep you warm and contains a little protein throughout the round. Make sure to buy a high-quality bone broth. Some are made with MSG and do not contain much collagen. Whether it is chicken or beef broth, it should be like Jello after being refrigerated. This indicates that there is a high amount of collagen in the broth. Lance Roll of the

Brothery makes great chicken and beef broth. I've visited his brothery, and he takes no short cuts. You can purchase his high-quality delicious broth from *http://www.bonebroth.com.* He ships directly all across the United States.

You've talked about cortisol levels. I don't know if I have high or low levels. How can I get tested?

Testing cortisol levels is a simple process. It's a collection of saliva at four times during the day. The time periods are upon rising, lunchtime, late afternoon, and before sleep. This gives a snapshot of cortisol levels throughout a typical day. It's important to know the levels through-out the day because cortisol levels should be high in the morning then slowly drop throughout the day. Often, cortisol levels are dysfunctional. This leads to fatigue, irritability, incomplete recovery, excessive soreness, sleep problems, and many other issues. Contact my office at *info@robertyang.net* if you would like to have your cortisol levels assessed. All testing can be done in the privacy of your home. Adrenal Stress Index test kits can be shipped internationally.

I know you're a big proponent of protein, especially in the form of animal protein, but I've chosen to be vegan. Is there another way to increase my protein intake?

Another way to increase your protein intake is with supplementation. There are many types of plant-based proteins such as rice, pea, and hemp. I know the "go-to" protein for vegans is to combine grains and legumes for a "complete" protein. This is true but a partial truth.

Yes, it does provide a complete protein with most of the essential amino acids, but there's some baggage that comes with this "complete" protein. The ratio of carbohydrates to protein is very skewed. For example, a cup of black beans and long-grain brown rice roughly contain 10 grams of protein and a whopping 45 grams of carbohydrates. For some of you, it may be too many carbohydrates that may put you on that roller coaster of blood sugar. For others, you may start to notice your pants become a bit tighter due to the excessive carb intake. It may be a better choice to go with the beans and forego the rice unless it's after a hard workout.

Is alcohol healthy for me?

There's a consensus that alcohol is healthy for you. The truth is that alcohol is not healthy. In fact, it's detrimental to your health and game. Regular alcohol consumption compromises digestion, screws up hormones, and disrupts your sleep.

As you drink alcohol, it creates dysfunction in the gastrointestinal (GI) tract. Digestion is disrupted in the stomach because of the suppression of hydrochloric acid (HCL). HCL is a critical acid to kill any pathogen you may have accidentally swallowed so it doesn't pass on to the small intestine. It's critical for the digestion of protein and absorption of B vitamins and minerals.

As alcohol moves on, it reaches the small intestine, which is a semipermeable membrane, meaning it may allow molecules to pass through it. The terrain of the small intestine is analogous to riot police. The riot police form a wall to prevent any rioter from bursting through the line. If a rioter throws a cocktail bomb at the wall, there's a hole in the wall.

In the same way, alcohol is the cocktail bomb (literally) that creates small holes in lining of the small intestine (a.k.a. leaky gut). Alcohol creates a leaky gut, allowing toxins and pathogens a free ticket to the bloodstream and other organs. Frequently, undigested foods can readily bypass the digestive tract and infiltrate the blood via this leaky gut. For this reason, University of Ottawa researchers say there's a FOUR-FOLD increase in allergic reactions to food when alcohol is consumed. All of these issues lead to an inflammatory effect. This is the reason why many players feel bloated after drinking alcohol.

Alcohol does a number on your hormones. Finnish researchers gave subjects two glasses of wine or four glasses of wine and tested growth hormone (GH) and thyroid-stimulating hormone (TSH). Growth hormone is a repair hormone as well as our natural fat-burning hormone that is produced predominately at night. Thyroid-stimulating hormone is an important hormone that regulates thyroid function and metabolism.

As subjects were sleeping, blood was collected throughout the night. The results demonstrated a significant decrease in TSH and GH. More specifically, four glasses of wine decreased GH by 80%, and two glasses of wine decreased GH by 63%! The more wine you drink, the less GH and TSH you produce. This has huge implications on recovery for players and is the main reason why people get fat when drinking wine.

Alcohol is one of the fastest-digesting substances we can consume. Therefore, when you have a glass with dinner, it puts you on a blood sugar roller coaster. As blood sugar plummets, cortisol is produced to normalize blood sugar. This is a homeostatic mechanism so that your blood sugar doesn't drop too low. However, cortisol is being produced at the absolute worst time. As you approach bedtime, cortisol should be at its lowest. This allows melatonin to be produced. Melatonin is called the "darkness" hormone that promotes sleep. Therefore, sleep is disrupted.

Some players have a difficult time falling asleep due to the lack of melatonin. Other players think they fall asleep very well with alcohol, but it's called paradoxical sleep. The severe drop in blood sugar makes them drowsy so they fall asleep. But many golfers wake up at 2:00 a.m. wondering why they're wide awake. This is a common scenario, because as blood sugar bottoms out, cortisol is produced. Remember that cortisol is a stimulating hormone. This wakes up a player.

Hopefully I've dissuaded you from drinking alcohol. If you do decide to drink alcohol, follow these guidelines. Make sure to drink a bottle of water before your drink. This will help to dilute the alcohol. Eat something to counter the effects of the alcohol. Consuming a meal with PFF will help a tremendous amount to blunt the blood sugar roller coaster of alcohol.

I travel quite a bit and find it's difficult to eat well on the road. Do you have any tips for eating when traveling?

Eating while traveling can be difficult. I remember one of my players calling me in a panic. He said the only restaurants available to him were McDonald's, Wendy's, and Taco Bell! I told this player to make the best decision in the situation given. For this particular player, it meant ordering a salad at McDonald's and a burger. I told him to eat the salad and throw away the hamburger buns and eat the burger patty. This may be an extreme situation, but it happens. Some players are playing mini-tours in small towns with low-quality food choices.

I used to get really stressed out about finding quality organic food when traveling. The anxiety I was experiencing was worse than eating nonorganic food. I was creating more stress to my body than the food I would eat! I no longer worry about food when I travel. I do the best I can in the situation. I want you to have the same mindset when you travel. Do the best that you can and follow these principles and you'll do fine.

Eating well on the road starts with hydration. The first priority should be water. When you get to your destination, look for a high-quality water. No matter how tired you are, plan on buying a few days' worth of water. Having water will allow you to start off the day with proper hydration. If you can't find a market nearby, look for a pharmacy. Most pharmacies are open late and have water you can purchase.

The most important aspect of eating is to follow the PFF principle. This will ensure your blood sugar is level. You can always order protein, fat, and fiber at any restaurant. Almost every single restaurant in world will have eggs and bacon as an option for breakfast. Simply add an apple and you have a PFF meal. Lunch is pretty simple too. Order a protein source such as chicken, fish, pork, or beef with steamed or sautéed vegetables. Add in a side salad with an oil and vinegar dressing, and you have a great PFF meal. Dinner will be similar to lunch but will be slightly different if you exercise toward the evening. A postexercise dinner should have a serving of starch such as rice or potato to facilitate recovery.

One tip that can make life easy in the morning is to eat dinner for breakfast. If you find a restaurant that you like with good food, then order two dinners. Eat one for dinner and take the other one to go for breakfast. You can reheat this in the morning in your hotel room and not have to worry about hunting around for a good breakfast place.

I'm going to be playing in extremely hot and humid environments. What should I do differently?

If you're going to play in hot and humid climates, make sure to drink half your body weight in ounces per day. Add one pinch of unrefined salt to every liter of water. This will be your base and foundation of hydration each day. To ensure that you're hydrating properly, weigh yourself without clothes before each round. Weigh yourself after each round. For every pound that you lose, drink 16 ounces of water to replenish the water loss. Remember, this extra water should be accompanied by salt.

I'm going on a golf trip and will be playing five days straight. Is there anything I can do at night to recharge for the next day?

Multiple days of golf can be a challenge, especially if you're not used to playing several days in a row. One of the best things you can do is to take an Epsom salt bath each night. Your skin is the largest organ in your body. Whatever you put on your skin means you're absorbing it!

Epsom salt is magnesium sulfate. Magnesium is involved in over 350 chemical processes in the body. In particular, magnesium helps reduce lactic acid and relax muscles. Fill up a bathtub with four to five cups of Epsom salts in warm water and soak for twenty minutes. This will help relieve muscle soreness and enhance sleep.

Magnesium is a calming mineral, so improving sleep will further enhance recovery each night before playing another round of golf.

I'm a collegiate player, and there are days when I play thirty-six holes in a day. It's a long day, and I start dragging toward the end of the round. What can I do to prevent this fatigue?

This can be a very tough situation for collegiate players. There's no magic formula for this particular situation. The PFF principle is even more important for a collegiate player. It's really important for a player to eat a big breakfast. This breakfast will be bigger than normal. The modification for breakfast is to increase proteins and fats.

Remember my story of eggs and bacon? This is a time to load up on eggs and bacon. Every player will be different, so it's important to experiment before trying this before a tournament. For example, if you're used to eating two whole eggs and two pieces of bacon before a round of golf, try increasing the eggs to three whole eggs and three pieces of bacon. If you feel good on this during a round, then go up to four whole eggs and four or five pieces of bacon. I would go beyond your threshold then back off slightly. What I mean is overeat on purpose. You'll know if you've overeaten, because you'll have a slight nauseated feeling. If you do get to this point, decrease the bacon by one strip and/or reduce one egg. Remember to add in veggies too, to increase the fiber content of this PFF meal.

One of the biggest issues a collegiate player will face is the box lunch. It normally consists of a sandwich, chips, cookie, and water. Not ideal for a player, because it's a heavily loaded with carbohydrates. There isn't enough food to sustain a player. The best option would be to pack extra food. Adding protein and fat is key for sustaining a player through the second round. Salami or bacon is a good add-on to a sandwich to keep blood sugar flatlined and hunger at a minimum. Another option is to buy corn tortillas and load them full of sandwich meat, along with bacon or avocado.

PART 4
Supplements

11
SUPPLEMENTS

Supplements are a polarizing topic. Some athletes and nutrition experts swear by them, while others think they're a complete waste of money. I fully believe some products work and make a positive difference for a hard-training athlete. Many players become distracted by supplement claims and ignore the fundamental basics to get results: high-quality nutrition, exercise, and sleep. These topics will never be very sexy, but they're the most important aspects of performance and health.

First, let's look at the definition of what a supplement is:

A supplement is something added to something else in order to complete or enhance it.

Food supplements are products that you add to an already solid nutrition program to make it even better. In other words, if you're not eating right, drinking enough water, sleeping well, and working out intensely, the supplements you take won't make much if any noticeable difference.

The following are some features to keep in mind when selecting a supplement.

Go After Health

Golfers tend to be interested in one thing: hitting the ball farther. Whenever I bring up the idea of health, I see players start to zone out, and their eyes begin to roll back into their heads. Health may seem like a boring topic, but it's so important for longevity and performance.

In 2006, *Golfer's Digest* surveyed golfers, finding that 80% of players suffered from some kind of injury, pain, or illness. Out of that group:

- 27% had low-back pain or injury
- 24% had allergies
- 23% had high blood pressure
- 22% had high cholesterol
- 22% had knee pain or injury

So almost 50% of these golfers have physical issues with the lower back and knees. The survey didn't even take into account golfer's elbow and shoulder issues that many players experience. If you're injured, you can't play, and if you can't play, you can't get better. Improve your health, and you'll feel better, have more energy, sleep better, and recover faster after each round of golf.

We Live in a Toxic World

Golf can make you sick.

Have you ever thought of what it takes to maintain a golf course and how they keep the greens so nice and pretty? There are massive amounts of chemicals that go into it — fertilizers, pesticides, and fungicides. Golfers are exposed to these chemicals by direct contact to the turf, inhaling vapors, and drinking contaminated groundwater.

A study titled "Toxic Fairways" was performed by the Office of the New York State Attorney General. The report looked at the groundwater contamination that can occur on Long Island's golf courses.

Here are some of the findings:

"The 52 golf courses reported using a total of approximately 200,000 pounds of bulk dry products and close to 9,000 gallons of bulk liquid formulations in one year. This included 192 different pesticide products containing 50 different active ingredients which totaled more than 50,000 pounds."

That's a lot of chemicals, to put it mildly. *The International Journal of Environmental Research and Public Health* has pointed to many of these chemicals as potential carcinogens (i.e., they may cause cancer), as well as being toxic to the nervous system and disruptive to your hormones. Worst of all, for the most part, contact with them when you're playing a round is unavoidable.

Now don't panic yet, because there's no conclusive proof these compounds are hazardous to human health, but it's logical to assume long-term exposure to them could be problematic. One way to fight back (aside from limiting your golf outings, which I would never ask you to do!) is to consume foods and supplements that help the body detoxify itself.

These days, with all the toxins we are exposed to, I don't think that food alone can cut it. I offer the following list of supplements to improve general health in the avid golfer.

Supplements Every Golfer Should Take

Probiotics

If you remember from the chapter on fiber and gut health, you have both good and bad bacteria living in your digestive tract. Researcher Fredrik Bäckhed says the gut is home to approximately 100,000,000,000,000 (that's 100 trillion if you can't count that high) micro-organisms. The Department of Primary Industries in Victoria, Australia, shows that the human gut is home to ten times more bacteria than there are cells in the entire body!

To quote the Greek physician Hippocrates, "All disease begins in the gut." Gut health is currently being looked at as the next frontier to help resolve chronic diseases, including diabetes, obesity, cardiovascular disease, depression, and autoimmune diseases. If there are more bad bacteria in your body, your digestion will get screwed up and your overall health will suffer.

- Factors that contribute to unhealthy gut bacteria are:
- medications such as antibiotics, NSAIDs, and birth control
- low fiber intake
- processed foods
- dietary toxins such as sugar and trans fatty acids
- stress
- chronic infections of bacteria, parasites, and/or candida
- excess alcohol intake

GEEK MOMENT: THE PROBLEM WITH ANTIBIOTICS

 Doctors prescribe antibiotics to kill bad bacteria that make you sick. The problem is the drugs can't discriminate in what they target, so they kill all the bacteria in your gut, both bad and good. Stanford researchers have shown that as little as three or four days of antibiotic use can dramatically change the amount and ratios of flora in your gut.

I used to recommend clients avoid taking probiotics while undergoing treatment with antibiotics. My logic was the antibiotics would kill off everything, so why bother taking probiotics — they'd just go to waste. But new research has proven me wrong. Researchers from the Journal of International Immunopharmacology performed a double-blind, placebo-controlled study with thirty subjects that had an infection of Helicobacter pylori. The control group was put on antibiotics for seven days but no probiotics. The experimental group was put on antibiotics for seven days but took probiotics. The control group that was not given probiotics showed an increase in bad bacteria. The probiotic group showed a decrease in bad bacteria and an increase in good bacteria.

There are times when antibiotics are necessary. Just make sure when you take antibiotics, you also take probiotics to help offset some of the damage they cause. You'll maintain healthy gut flora by allowing the "good" guys to proliferate.

Supplementing with probiotics ensures that your

digestive system stays in order. Probiotics are good bacteria that keep the gut healthy by making sure the bad guys don't get out of hand. These friendly bacteria have a number of important roles, including:

- Relieving symptoms of Irritable Bowel Syndrome (IBS)
- Improving digestion
- Producing vitamins
- Relieving symptoms of diarrhea
- Detoxifying chemicals
- Producing nutrients to repair the gut lining
- Help regulate immune function

They can also help with non-gut-related issues such as:
- skin conditions like eczema, psoriasis, and atopic dermatitis
- urinary and vaginal health,
- allergies,
- oral health

Lactobacillus and bifidobacterium are the most common probiotics. Both can be found in yogurt and other fermented foods such as sauerkraut, kimchi, and kombucha. Probiotic supplements come in powder form or in capsules. Since the bacteria are alive, it's important to keep probiotic supplements refrigerated.

The number of bacteria in one capsule is in the billions. I recommend a probiotic with at a minimum of 20 billion CFUs. Take one caplet on an empty stomach first thing in the morning for best absorption. If you're taking any antibiotics to fight an infection, triple the dose and maintain it for a month after stopping the antibiotic treatment.

Fish Oil

Oil from fish contains omega-3 fatty acids. To recap, the body needs both omega-6 and omega-3 fats. This ratio can be highly out of whack for those individuals that eat a highly processed diet. A skewed omega 6:3 ratio may lead to excess inflammation in the body. Just remember that any condition ending in an "itis" is an inflammatory condition. For instance, tendonitis is an inflammation of a tendon. If a tendon or ligamentous structure is inflamed due to injury, the lack of omega-3s can exacerbate the condition. Reducing the omega 6:3 ratio can reduce overall body inflammation and help reduce inflammation in joints.

GEEK MOMENT: FATS FOR JOINTS

 Rheumatoid arthritis (RA) causes stiffness and pain in joints and can be a very debilitating disease. One of the answers to this pain and discomfort is to use nonsteroidal anti-inflammatory drugs (NSAIDs) to reduce the inflammation. However, NSAIDS are a double-edged sword because they are known to cause side effects to the gastrointestinal tract, liver, and kidneys.

Now, what if we could use something to treat inflammation that's natural and doesn't have any side effects? This is where essential fatty acids (EFAs) come into play. Research in the Annals of Rheumatic Disease showed the benefit of EFAs with RA patients. When subjects were given evening primrose oil (EPO), another omega-6 fat, and fish oil, twelve out of fifteen people were able to reduce or end their NSAID use inside of fifteen months.

You may be thinking, "I eat plenty of fish. So I don't need to take fish oils." Eating fish several times a week does help increase omega-3's in the body, provided that you're eating the right type of fish. Salmon can be a nutritional Jekyll and Hyde. It's the most frequently eaten fish because of the high amounts of omega-3s versus omega-6s. However, it depends on how the salmon are raised.

Salmon farming began in the late 1980s due to the growing demand, but there's a big issue. The salmon were no longer the same. When the fish were cut open, the flesh was gray instead of the bright reddish-orange flesh typically seen in salmon. The reddish-orange color comes from the crustaceans (shrimp or krill) that salmon eat, but the diet of farm-raised salmon was drastically changed. Salmon farmers were using fish pellets made up of soy, canola, and corn. That is not the normal diet of a salmon. To remedy this issue, the farmers gave the salmon canthaxanthin or astaxanthin to create the "appealing" salmon color.

The omega-6:3 ratio content was drastically reduced due to this change in diet. Unfortunately, if you primarily eat farm-raised salmon or other fish, you're not getting any omega-3s, and you're putting yourself into a more inflamed state. This is where fish oil supplementation can help to balance this ratio.

There are two ways to take fish oil: capsules or liquid. If you have bad memories of Mom forcing you to take nasty cod liver oil, capsules may be the best option for you. The only downside to taking capsules is that you need a lot of them to get the right dosage. Since fish oil is sensitive to heat and light, the capsules are made to protect the oil from going bad, but a capsule can only carry a small amount of fish oil (typically only half a gram).

Consuming fish oil as a liquid is more economical, and these days, oils are flavored with lemon or orange, so you don't have to worry about the taste or "fish burps" afterward. Another option is to use fish oil products in smoothie form. They taste quite amazing and leave no fishy aftertaste.

My recommendation for fish oil is one gram per 50 pounds of your body weight. See the chart below to find the dosage you need.

Weight in pounds	Capsules of fish oil	Teaspoons of liquid oil	Teaspoons of smoothie fish oil
100	4 capsules	2 teaspoons	2 teaspoons
150	6 capsules	3 teaspoons	3 teaspoons
200	8 capsules	4 teaspoons	4 teaspoons
250	10 capsules	5 teaspoons	5 teaspoons

Always take fish oil with food, which helps the digestion and absorption. I recommend splitting up the dosage between breakfast and dinner. If you are 200 pounds, you should take four capsules of fish oil (or four teaspoons of liquid) with breakfast and then again at dinner.

Make sure that you are buying high-quality fish oil supplements. Some supplement manufacturers are just out there to make a quick buck and aren't concerned about the quality of the fish oil. When consuming fish, we have to be careful about heavy metals and other chemicals. It's even more important with fish oils, since they're a highly concentrated form of fat.

Since fish oil products are concentrated products, purity is of utmost concern. A high-quality fish oil product is molecular distilled and filtered to minimize chances of heavy metals, pesticides, solvents, PCBs, and other contaminants.

Vitamin D

Vitamin D is a hot topic in nutrition, since many people have been discovered to be deficient in it. The name vitamin D is a bit of a misnomer because it goes way beyond being just a vitamin. Specifically, it's a seco-steroid — a hormone in the body. The interesting thing is that you don't even need to consume this vitamin. Your body can produce all it needs if you get enough exposure to the sun.

This is why, on paper, it sounds easy to get vitamin D, but it's not quite that simple. In the twentieth century, a deficiency of vitamin D in childhood would cause a malformation of bone called rickets. Current literature suggest that the role of vitamin D goes way beyond bones, and it has been shown to be critical for:

- calcium regulation
- communication between cells
- hormonal effects
- immune system support
- blood sugar control
- regulating blood pressure

Vitamin D is produced in the skin. Once the UVB rays from the sun hit the skin, cholesterol (7-dehydrocholesterol) is converted to vitamin D. It can also be derived from food, including animal foods such as liver, eggs, sardines, herring, and salmon. However, most people turn their noses up at foods such as sardines and liver, so the consumption of vitamin D from whole food sources has decreased dramatically over the years. Fortified foods such as cereals, bread, and orange juice also have vitamin D. But while these foods contain vitamin D, they're processed and contain little other nutrition. It's not worth eating processed foods just for the vitamin D. Furthermore, the amount added to these foods is minuscule anyway.

The Recommended Dietary Allowance (RDA) of vitamin D for adults is 600 IU per day. This is the amount that is necessary to avoid rickets, but it's not enough to promote maximum health and performance.

Ask your doctor to check your vitamin D levels the next time you get blood work done. The marker is 25 Hydroxy D {25(OH)D}. Most research points to optimal levels being between 50–60 ng/ml per day. On average, it requires a dose of 4,000 to 10,000 IU per day to achieve these levels in the blood.

Take note: even if you spend a lot of time in the sun, that doesn't mean your body is making enough vitamin D. There are many factors that affect the production of vitamin D.

The angle of the sun has a lot to do with how UVB rays affect you. The closer you live to the equator, the less of an angle the sun has to shine on you and the more UVB rays that directly hit you for vitamin D production. So, if you live in Hawaii for example, your body will produce more vitamin D. On the other hand, if you live in Anchorage, Alaska, you will not produce much at all.

The time of the day you are in the sun has an impact as well. Most dermatologists say to avoid the sun between 10:00 a.m. and 2:00 p.m. because this is the window where the most skin damage occurs, but it's also the best time for vitamin D production. You want to be out in the sun when it is directly overhead. An easy way to think about this is the longer your shadow, the less vitamin D you are making.

GEEK MOMENT: 20/20

 A good rule of thumb that I learned from Dr. James Cannell, founder of the Vitamin D Council, is the 20/20 rule. The body has the capacity to produce 20,000 IU of vitamin D in twenty minutes of exposure. It doesn't take very long for your body to produce a significant amount of vitamin D. As long as you give it some exposure. If you plan on a round of golf at 10:00 a.m., then hold off on the sunscreen. Expose as much of your skin to the sun as you play for fifteen to twenty minutes then put on sunscreen. At least you get some exposure then protect yourself from burning the rest of the round.

Sunscreen is the big monkey wrench we throw into vitamin D production. A sunscreen with an SPF of 8 has been shown to block out 95% of UVB rays. Most people use a stronger SPF than that, which blocks all UVB rays. For these reasons, it's best to get your vitamin D from a blend of foods, sunshine, and supplementation. As mentioned earlier, it takes an average daily dose of 4,000 IU–10,000 IU of vitamin D to obtain adequate levels of vitamin D in the body.

Magnesium

Calcium is the mineral that receives a lot of attention

when it comes to bones. However, magnesium is a mineral that is primarily found in bones and soft tissues. More importantly, it plays a part in over 350 reactions in the body. It's intimately involved in the production of adenosine triphosphate (ATP), the energy source for your cells.

Besides low energy, magnesium deficiency may show up as:

- high blood pressure
- anxiety
- chronic fatigue
- muscle cramps
- cravings for chocolate (seriously)
- constipation

Magnesium is part of a pigment called chlorophyll, the stuff that makes plants green. Therefore, green, leafy vegetables are the highest sources of magnesium. Nuts are a good source of magnesium too.

There are several factors that will influence your levels of magnesium. One is eating less of it. For most people in the modern world, green vegetables have been replaced in the diet by grains and dairy products.

Another factor is chronic stress, which can come from the following sources:

- job
- family
- too much sugar
- hot and humid weather
- junk food
- alcohol
- lack of sleep
- death of a loved one
- exercise

The list could go on and on. We are bombarded by stress. Researchers at the Military Medical Academy in Belgrade, Serbia, have shown chronic stress leads to decreases in both free and total magnesium concentrations. As a result, most people are magnesium-deficient.

To see where you stand, use a simple magnesium load test. Take a magnesium supplement until you get the runs. It's crude, I admit, but highly effective. I digress. You won't get the runs like you would taking a laxative. You'll notice that your stools will be much softer and more watery when you've taken too much magnesium. Magnesium is a water-soluble mineral, so your body gets rid of the excess via the stool.

Refer to the table below to see how to incrementally increase your magnesium intake.

Start with one capsule at breakfast and dinner. Stay at that dose for three days. If you notice your stools becoming very soft to the point of being a pile of mush, back off by one capsule. But I've rarely seen this happen.

Day	Breakfast	Dinner
1-3	1 cap	1 cap
4-6	1 cap	2 caps
7-9	2 caps	2 caps
10-12	2 caps	3 caps
13-15	3 caps	3 caps
16-18	3 caps	4 caps
19-21	4 caps	4 caps
22-24	4 caps	5 caps
25-27	5 caps	5 caps

Let's say you are on day sixteen through eighteen, and after taking three capsules in the morning and four capsules at night, you have soft, runny stool for several days. Reduce the magnesium to three capsules with breakfast and three with dinner. This should normalize the stool. This would be your dosage unless the stool softens again. Then you would reduce the magnesium by one capsule.

Don't be surprised if you end up taking ten capsules per day. Just remember that the more stress you have, the more magnesium your body will need. Monitor your stool, and that will let you know when to back off on magnesium.

I had a client who was an attorney, a highly competitive master level triathlete, and had an issue with energy and constipation. Once she found the right amount of magnesium, she had daily bowel movements and an increase in energy. Several months later, she complained of missing bowel movements and a drop in energy. At this point in her life, she was actively involved in a big case in court and training for the Ironman in Hawaii. These challenges were overloading her with mental, emotional, and physical stress. I had her increase her magnesium levels again, and her stools normalized and she regained her energy. She also noticed that her tolerance to stress increased as well.

There are many forms of magnesium. The most effective form I have found is magnesium bisglycinate chelate. It's chelated, which means it's a more absorbable form of magnesium than other ones. Use the magnesium load chart to determine your ideal dose.

GEEK MOMENT: MAGNESIUM GLYCINATE CHELATE

Magnesium is typically in the form of magnesium oxide. When consumed, it raises the pH in the small intestine. This creates an environment that inhibits the absorption of magnesium. Therefore, the amount of magnesium oxide is typically higher. Magnesium bisglycinate chelate has two glycine molecules that occupy sites on the magnesium molecule that reduces the acidity of the intestine and helps improve absorption.

Branched-Chain Amino Acids

As we covered in the protein section, branched-chain amino acids (BCAAs) are three specific aminos: leucine, isoleucine, and valine. They're three of the nine essential amino acids that your body needs. "Essential" means that you need to eat them to get them into your system.

I learned about the use of BCAAs many years ago from a mentor of mine, Eric Serrano, M.D. He's a big proponent of the use of BCAAs pre-, intra-, and post-workout. BCAAs are unlike any other amino acid in the body. They're considered an "ergogenic" supplement, meaning that they help with performance, stamina, and/or recovery. BCAA use is one way to maintain strength and power over the course of eighteen holes. Muscle cells oxidize BCAAs as a source of cellular energy, i.e., ATP.

I like using BCAAs with players because they reduce muscle soreness. Research from the *Journal of the*

International Society of Sports Nutrition looked at nation-al-level rugby players. Researchers randomly gave one group of subjects BCAAs and the other group a placebo. They performed five sets of twenty drop-jumps. Each ath-lete was instructed to step off a two-foot box and then immediately jump vertically with maximal effort. Even for trained athletes, that's a lot of jumping! Researchers mea-sured the amount of muscle damage, and the BCAA group showed significantly lower levels than the placebo group.

One issue with training golfers is the lack of an off-season for a PGA or LPGA player. A professional golfer could potentially play every single week of the year. Since there's no off-season as in other sports, training for strength and power can be difficult. This kind of training can produce a lot of soreness. A player can't afford to be too sore to practice and play well.

I have my golfers use BCAAs before, during, and/or after training. They'll be less sore and be able to train more often (and practice more, too). The gain in strength and power means more distance off the tee.

GEEK MOMENT: BCAAS PREVENT MENTAL FATIGUE

 Besides their affects on muscles, BCAAs can fight fatigue in your brain. During exercise the amount of amino acids fluctuates. University of Oxford researchers have shown the amino acid trypto-phan tends to rise in the blood while the levels of BCAAs decrease. The increased ratio of trypto-phan:BCAAs leads to an increased transport of tryptophan across the blood brain barrier (BBB).

Tryptophan is the precursor to 5-hydroxytryptamine (5-HT) in the brain; 5-HT is what many of you know as serotonin, the "feel-good" neurotransmitter. However, it's also the sleep promoter — not an ideal situation when you want to be focused during a round of golf. Supplemental amounts ensure that enough BCAAs enter the BBB versus tryptophan, keeping the chemical balance in favor of your mind staying sharp rather than calming down and vegging out.

BCAAs come mainly from animal protein. Dr. Loren Cordain, the author of The Paleo Diet For Athletes, says that lean proteins such as meat, fish, and eggs contain the highest amount of BCAAs. This is why you should be eating a significant amount of animal foods, but supplementation makes a big impact too.

The big difference lies in the absorption. Think of chicken breast as a train and BCAA supplements as separate railroad cars. The train is made up of several cars that are connected together. In the same way, chicken is made up of several types of amino acids that are connected by peptide bonds. In order for your body to utilize BCAAs, it must first break down the peptide bonds. This takes several hours of digestion.

BCAA supplements are just the separate railroad cars. Therefore, the body can utilize them quickly. Very quickly! In fact, Richard Lord, the author of *Laboratory Evaluations for Integrative and Functional Medicine*, has shown that 5 grams of amino acids doubles the amount of aminos in the blood within 30 minutes. So taking amino acids 30 minutes before training is the optimal time to increase the supply to the muscles and the brain.

The dose of BCAAs depends on the weight of the athlete. The more you weigh, the more you need. Use the following chart to determine your BCAA intake.

Bodyweight (pounds)	BCAA Intake
140	4 grams
160	8 grams
180	12 grams
200	16 grams

Since it takes about thirty minutes for the levels of amino acids to flood the bloodstream, it's best to time the intake of the BCAAs. If I have a player scheduled for a workout at 8:00 a.m., I calculate the time they should be drinking the amino acids. For example, an LPGA player has an hour workout that consists of fifteen minutes of a warmup and forty-five minutes of lifting. I'll have her start drinking her BCAAs at 7:45 a.m. to ensure that her muscles are bathed in amino acids to use as an energy source during her lifting session.

I like to use BCAA Powder with L-Glutamine from Designs for Health. It has a good ratio of leucine, isoleucine, and valine that totals 2.5 grams of BCAAs per teaspoon. In addition, each teaspoon contains 2 grams of glutamine. Glutamine is another "conditionally" essential amino acid. This means that the body can make it, but in certain conditions it becomes essential.

In times of stress, trauma, and illness, glutamine becomes an essential amino acid as the normal supplies are being used up rapidly. It's the most abundant amino acid in skeletal muscle, but it has nothing to do with muscles. The primary reason why I recommend it is the influence it has on the immune system. It's the primary fuel source for the cells of the small intestine and immune system.

Researchers in England have shown the recovery period after high-intensity intermittent exercise can create falling levels of glutamine in the blood. In addition to exercise, other stress causes a release of cortisol, which requires a need for glutamine for gluconeogenesis (energy production).

If you had a perfect diet, had no stress, and only worked out, then you might not need glutamine. However, the cumulative effect of stress in the form of golf practice, gym workouts, and daily life stressors requires the need for glutamine post exercise. The combination of BCAA Powder with L-Glutamine is a great synergistic amino acid product that can help with recovery and help support the immune system postexercise.

12
FAQS ABOUT
SUPPLEMENTS

I have an annual checkup, and my doctor has checked my vitamin D levels and said I was fine. It was 30 ng/mL and the range is 30-100 ng/ML. Should I be concerned that it's at the low end?

Reference levels are just that, a reference. There's a low and high end when it comes to blood values. The level of 30 ng/mL is in the normal range but is considered low/normal. Yes, it's in the reference range, but it's not optimal, especially in the context of bone and muscle strength. According to Dr. Robert Heaney of Creighton University, the optimal blood levels of should be 50–60 ng/mL. The standard recommendation is 2,000 IU per day. However, the dose of 2,000 IU is insufficient to bring the levels up to 50-60 ng/mL. This is why I recommend 4,000–10,000 IU of vitamin D per day to achieve optimal levels. In fact, a study by the department of endocrinology of St. George Hospital in Australia showed subjects who were given a dose of 5,000 IU of vitamin D versus 2,000 IU showed an overall greater increase in vitamin D levels. Start at 5,000–6,000 IU per day and have your doctor recheck you in six months. If the levels are within 50–60 ng/mL, then stay at that dose. If the levels are still below 50 ng/mL, increase to 8000 IU. Recheck in six months and fine-tune if necessary.

Since vitamin D is a fat-soluble vitamin, isn't toxicity a concern with the higher doses?

There's always a concern for toxicity with any added nutrient. You can take too much of anything. The Tolerable Upper Intake Level (UL) was established by the Food and Nutrition Board (FNB) as 2,000 IU per day. However, this was established in 1997. Updated research by the *American Journal of Clinical Nutrition* has established the UL as 10,000 IU per day with no toxicity. So rest assured that the higher doses I recommend are completely safe. If you're still concerned, then testing your vitamin D levels every six months is the only way to know if you're taking too much vitamin D.

I've heard that sunscreens can be toxic to the skin. Do you have any recommendations for a high-quality sunscreen?

Whatever you put on your skin, you're eating it! Your skin is a living, breathing organ that absorbs anything you put on it. Therefore, you should choose a sunscreen with minimal toxic ingredients. The Environmental Working Group (EWG) has a great website called Skin Deep (https://www.ewg.org/skindeep/#.Wyb2dS2ZPOQ).

They rate many of the sunscreens on the market from least to most toxic. It's great guide to choose the least toxic sunscreen.

Are whole foods such as yogurt, sauerkraut, and kimchi enough of a probiotic to help my digestion?

I'm a big fan of fermented foods for digestive health. It's a preventative way to keep the "good guys" winning the battle over the "bad guys." So keep eating those fermented foods. If you have significant digestive issues such as constipation, diarrhea, bloating, gas, and/or pain, fermented foods may or may not help. The amount of probiotics is measured in colony-forming units (CFUs). Sometimes the fermented food doesn't have enough CFUs to repopulate the intestinal tract, so you may need to supplement with a probiotic. A probiotic should have a minimum of 10 billion CFUs to gain any digestive benefit. In severe digestive cases, I may recommend up to 100 billion CFUs a day.

I can remember the days of my mom forcing cod liver down my throat, and the thought of choking down any liquid or custard makes me want to vomit. So I choose to take capsules. The problem is that I get fish burps! It's really disgusting. Is there anything I can do to prevent this?

The biggest reason is rancid fish oil. Sometimes companies use poor sources of fish oil that have gone rancid. If you find a company that sells fish at a price that is too good to be true, then it is. If you've bought from a reputable company and still get fish burps, use this little trick: keep the fish oils in the refrigerator. This usually does the trick. If not, then you may need to have your digestion assessed for enzymes.

If I perform the magnesium load test, do I have to worry about running to the bathroom?

No. Magnesium is a water-soluble mineral, so if your body is overloaded, it excretes the excess in the stool. There won't be any immediate laxative effect. You'll simply notice a change in stool that is loose or possibly watery at worst.

I've seen BCAAs in capsules, tablets, and powder. What's the best form?

Powder is the most convenient form to take high amounts of BCAAs. Capsules and tablets have an upper limit of 500 mg of BCAAs. You'll be taking gram dosages, so you would have to take a minimum of eight capsules at a time. This can be quite disruptive, since you have to swallow capsules during a training session. Powder is easily mixed into water and can be sipped throughout a workout session.

It was recommended I drink a protein shake during a tournament for energy. Could BCAAs replace the protein shake?

I would prefer that players consume BCAAs rather than a protein shake. As mentioned earlier, any protein powder must first be broken down to individual amino acids before the body can absorb and utilize the amino acids. This can take several hours. Powdered BCAAs don't require digestion and can be in the bloodstream within thirty minutes of consuming them. This has huge advantages for energy production for muscles, preventing muscle soreness, as well as mental concentration. In addition, I notice that players don't feel hungry when drinking BCAAs. This is a great side benefit, since hunger could be distracting to a player during a tournament. I would recommend doubling the standard dosage for workouts and drink it throughout a round of golf.

PART 5
Hole-in-One
Nutrition
User's
Manual

13
WHAT TO MAKE
OF ALL THIS

This is the most important section of the book and the moment you've been waiting for: the how-to guide for eating to be a better golfer.

You've learned the "why" behind my recommendations, but it doesn't really matter unless you know how to apply the knowledge to your everyday life. If you are willing to change and put in the effort with your nutrition, you will see results on the course — and, more importantly, in the way you look and feel.

I feel like an infomercial pitchman when I say this, but "results will vary from golfer to golfer." Some players I've worked with notice a difference in a matter of days. Others see slow and gradual changes over three to four weeks. Give your body a minimum of thirty days to let these changes take effect. Results may vary, but no matter who you are, results will come.

Changes in nutrition will improve your life in ways you've probably never even considered. For example, your sleep. As mentioned earlier, cortisol is a hormone that can be normalized by proper hydration and nutrition.

Time and time again, I have seen many players improve their sleep at night just by controlling blood sugar. The most common comment is: "I don't know if this makes sense, but ever since you've changed my food intake, I lie down at night, and I'm out cold and sleep like a log!"

When you control your blood sugar, you help to normalize cortisol levels. When cortisol levels are normalized, melatonin can work properly at night, promoting deep sleep.

Failing to Plan Is Planning to Fail

Whether you're part of a sports team, a company, or a military unit, everybody needs a plan to be successful. Nutrition is no different. Unless you know how you can make healthy food a regular part of your busy life, you won't. Let's start with a list of foods that should be in your refrigerator at all times. If you don't buy it, you won't eat it. Conversely, if you buy junk food, it's going to be eaten in place of the good stuff.

But First, a Quick Word About Cheating...

I'm not asking you to live like a monk. You can have your cake and eat it too — literally. Just not all the time.

For instance, I love mint chip ice cream (the one with small chocolate chips), but I don't eat it everyday. You can eat the foods you enjoy, even junk food, but you've got to eat the good stuff first. I'm a 90/10 type of guy. I eat well 90% of the time and eat whatever I want 10% of the time. As long as you stick to that 90%, your body won't even notice the 10%.

Let's do the math. If you eat five meals per day, that equates to thirty-five meals per week. Ten percent of thirty-five meals is three and half meals per week. That's three meals and a snack you can have per week that are completely off the program.

Many people call these indulgence meals "cheat meals," but I would rather call it a splurge meal. The word "cheat" makes you think of dishonesty. Some preliminary research says being stressed out about the food you eat has worse effects on you than a donut you ate. When you have a food that is off the plan, enjoy it! No need to stress about it. Think of it as splurging on yourself. Indulge in your pizza or ice cream then get back on the plan.

Food Shopping List

Any of these foods listed are fair game. You will see there is very little packaged food. Focus on eating whole foods close to the way they appear in nature.

When shopping for protein sources:
- Buy wild fish whenever possible
- Invest in grass-fed beef and game meat whenever possible
- Buy organic poultry whenever possible
- Seek out free-range eggs whenever possible

Fish	Shellfish	Meat	
Ahi tuna	Crab	Bacon (<1 gram carb/ serving)	
Cod	Lobster	Beef	
Flounder	Mussels	Buffalo	
Halibut	Oysters	Chicken (breast, leg, thigh)	
Mahi-mahi	Shrimp	Deer	
Orange roughy		Elk	
Salmon		Hen	
Sea bass		Lamb (chops, roast)	
Swordfish		Ostrich	
Tilapia		Pork (chops, roast)	
Trout		Quail	
Tuna		Turkey (breast, leg, thigh)	

When shopping for carbohydrate sources:
- Buy organic veggies and fruits when possible
- Eat vegetables at every meal (except postworkout)
- Eat fruits one to two times per day as a snack with proteins
- Eat starch items after exercise

Vegetable	Fruit	Starches
Alfalfa sprouts	Apples	Basmati rice
Artichokes	Avocado	Brown rice
Arugula	Banana	Corn on the cob
Asparagus	Blackberries	Cream of rice
Bamboo shoots	Cantaloupe	Gluten-free bread
Bok choy	Coconut	Jasmine rice
Broccoli	Grapefruit	Oatmeal (GF)
Brussels sprouts	Lemons	Potato
Cabbage	Oranges	Quinoa
Carrots	Olives	Red potato
Cauliflower	Peaches	Sweet potato
Celery	Pineapple	Tortillas (corn, rice)
Chard	Raspberries	Wild rice
Chives	Strawberries	Yams
Collard greens	Tomato	
Cucumbers	Watermelon	
Eggplant		
Endive		
Green beans		
Kale		
Leeks		
Lettuce		
Mushrooms		
Onions		
Peas		
Radicchio		
Red and green peppers		
Sauerkraut		
Snap peas		
Spinach		
Squash		
Zucchini		

When shopping for fats:

- Whenever possible, choose organic oils. Toxins are stored in fat, so buy organic.
- Nuts and seeds are often referred to as protein sources, but their protein is not complete. Rely on them as sources of fat instead.

Cooking oils	Nuts	Seeds	Other
Avocado oil	Almonds	Flax	Avocado
Butter	Cashews	Hemp	
Coconut oil	Macadamia	Pumpkin	
Lard	Pecans	Sunflower	
Olive oil	Peanut butter (legumes	Tahini	
Palm oil	Walnut		
Peanut oil			

GEEK MOMENT: GRANDMA KNEW BEST!

 Back in the day, it was common to see your grandma cooking bacon then collecting the fat to use later. Lard sounds bad, but it really isn't. Dr. Mary Enig, author of *Know Your Fats*, states that the fatty acid breakdown of lard is 50% monounsaturated, 40% saturated, 10% polyunsaturated. Since it's predominantly a monounsaturated fat, Enig says it should be classified as a monounsaturated fat, but the government calls it saturated fat and says you should avoid it. I say eat it. Lard contains palmitoleic acid, which is an antimicrobial. So not only is lard heart-healthy, it can also protect you from becoming sick. Save that bacon fat!

How Much Should I Eat?

I don't expect you to count calories and start weighing your food. I used to have clients do this. Counting calories drove them crazy, or they just gave up on following a plan entirely. You don't need to make your eating an exact science; you just need to follow a few guidelines to get the nutrition you need without overeating.

The first food you should put on your plate at every meal is protein. Eat one serving of protein at breakfast, lunch, and dinner. One serving of protein is the size of a deck of cards. When you don't eat enough protein, you'll probably know. The signs include:

- Feeling hungry within an hour after eating
- Craving sweets
- Developing slight headaches throughout the day
- Losing focus and concentration
- Feeling tired after eating a meal
- Overeating at night
- Suffering chronic muscle soreness for several days after workouts
- Sore and achy joints
- Use the following guide to help you determine your protein intake for the day.
- Protein serving = the size of deck of cards (approximately 20–25 grams of protein)

Bodyweight (pounds)	Amount of protein a day
100	3 decks
125	4 decks
150	5 decks
175	6 decks
200	7 decks

This serves as a starting point. If you have any of the symptoms listed above, you may need to experiment and increase your intake by one deck per day.

Your protein should be spread throughout the day. You shouldn't starve through the day and end up force-feeding yourself a cow for dinner. If you're 170 pounds, this is how you should divide your protein: Eat two decks' worth at breakfast, lunch, and dinner on nonworkout days. If you do work out, take one deck away from lunch or dinner and have that in the form of BCAAs before the workout or a protein shake after the workout. (Examples to follow).

More is not better. The classic sign that you have eaten too much protein is feeling nauseous. If that happens, back off on the protein.

GEEK MOMENT: STOP DRINKING PROTEIN SHAKES FOR BREAKFAST!

 Blending up a protein shake first thing in the morning seems like a good breakfast option. It's easy, and you can take it on the go. It's become trendy among people who don't even work out.

But here's the problem. Since the shake is liquid, it digests quickly and passes through your system fast. It may be fine before a workout to give you quick energy or postworkout to jump-start recovery. However, it's not the best way to start your day before a round of golf.

I've found that golfers feel hungry after a protein smoothie, and their blood sugar is not as
stable after lunch. Try to make the time to eat
a whole-food meal that's packed with protein to
establish level blood sugar for the day.

For those of you moaning and groaning because
I took away your breakfast smoothie, you'll find
a recipe under 10 Quick Breakfast Options that
uses the PFF principle when making a smoothie.

After you place your "deck" of protein on the plate,
your second focus should be vegetables. Here's my highly
technical guide to how to portion your vegetable serving
… eat as many as you want.

Your high-density glucose (HDG) carbs (think
starches like potatoes and rice) should only be eaten in
and around exercise. You should have these carbs within
an hour after finishing exercise, games, or practice. If you
feel like you're a bit sluggish during workouts, add another
serving to the last meal you have prior to exercise. Use
your closed fist to gauge servings. Start with half a fist's
worth and adjust from there to find what works for you.

Carbohydrate serving = the size of your fist

Amount of exercise	Serving of HDG Carbs postexercise
30 min	.5 fist
60 min	1 fist
90 min	1.5 fists
120 min	2 fists

Fat should be the last addition to your plate. But before you slather your veggies with butter, keep one thing in mind. Great protein sources such as beef, chicken, fish, and pork also contain fat. Even when you stick to the leanest sources, there's still going to be some fat in your protein, so you need to take this into consideration.

Red meat, whole eggs, and chicken thighs have higher amounts of fat, so there's no need to add fat. However, if you're eating low-fat protein sources such as egg whites, chicken breast, turkey breast, and lean fish, you should add fat to your plate.

Apart from the health benefits of fats, they also support satiety. The feeling of fullness and satisfaction prevents you from overeating in subsequent meals.

I was working with a professional athlete who was constantly ravenous. His coach told me he thought the guy might have a tapeworm! The athlete ate breakfast, but an hour later at practice he would be hungry. He would run off the field between plays to eat food. After analyzing his diet, I discovered this athlete wasn't eating fat at breakfast. He ate egg-white omelettes with turkey breast, along with veggies and fruit. After I had him switch to whole eggs at breakfast and adding fat to other meals, his appetite came under control. If this describes you after eating a meal, you need to add more fat to it. Start with one serving.

Fat serving size = one thumb size

Cooking your meats and veggies with fats is a great way to add fat to a meal. Butter, coconut oil, or olive oil are fine options. Alternatively, a small handful of nuts or quarter of an avocado would be great.

Hole-in-One Nutrition Principles

Here's a summary of all the eating advice I've given so far. Tack it to your fridge or carry it with you throughout the day, and you'll never be lost about what to eat or when.

- Drink half your body weight in ounces of water per day. Remember, all other fluids DO NOT count toward this intake.

- Always drink 25% of your total water intake first thing in the morning. As explained earlier in the hydration section, water has a major affect on your cognition, especially first thing in the morning. It's the best way to get you going in the morning. And I'm not just talking about energy. I've found drinking this much water is a great way to cleanse your system. It helps you urinate but keeps you regular too.

- Eat breakfast within an hour of getting up. No if, ands, or buts.

- Load up on PFF. A breakfast such as a vegetable omelette is a perfect example. Eggs have protein and fat, and the vegetables have fiber. Eating this type of breakfast will ensure level blood sugar before you head out to the course (or the office).

- Maintain level blood sugar throughout the day by eating PFF. Once you've established level blood sugar with breakfast, think of PFF throughout the day to avoid the blood sugar roller coaster.

- Eat a postexercise meal or shake within an hour of finishing an exercise session. This is the time to eat starches such as white rice, potatoes, and quinoa to help facilitate recovery and to replete your body.

- Level your blood sugar before bed. As you start to wind down toward the evening, you want to prepare your body for optimal sleep. Avoid high-sugar foods and eat a snack of PFF. This will ensure stable blood sugar for proper hormones to enhance sleep and recovery.

- Below are some sample meal plans to show how you can time meals around exercise or golf. Use them as a template, but feel free to sub in any of the foods from the shopping list I made you for variety.

Sample Meal Plan for Morning Exercise

Time	Meal	Food
6:30 a.m.	Hydration	25% of total water intake first thing upon rising
7:00 a.m.	Breakfast	Denver omelette (diced ham, green and red peppers cooked in coconut oil or butter) Strawberries
8:30–9:30 a.m.	Exercise	Water with pinch of unrefined salt and BCAAs
10:00 a.m.	Postworkout Meal #1	Whey protein shake Half-cup pineapple juice Half-cup frozen strawberries
11:30 a.m.	Postworkout/ Game Meal #2	Brown rice tortilla wrap Turkey breast slices Mustard Romaine lettuce
3:00 p.m.	Snack	Almonds and one apple
6:00 p.m.	Dinner	Blackened salmon Steamed asparagus
8:30 p.m.	Snack	Tuna salad with celery and carrot sticks

If you're a golfer who needs to lose weight, just have the protein powder postworkout.

If you're a golfer who needs to gain weight, double the juice and strawberries postworkout.

Sample Meal Plan for Morning Golf

Time	Meal	Food
6:30 a.m.	Hydration	25% of total water intake first thing upon rising
7:00 a.m.	Breakfast	Denver omelette (diced ham, green and red peppers cooked in coconut oil or butter) BACON Strawberries
8:30–12:30 p.m.	Golf	Water with pinch of unrefined salt and BCAAs and snacks on the course
12:30 p.m.	Postgolf Meal	Brown rice tortilla wrap Turkey breast slices Mustard Romaine lettuce
3:00 p.m.	Snack	Almonds and one apple
6:00 p.m.	Dinner	Blackened salmon Steamed asparagus
8:30 p.m.	Snack	Tuna salad with celery and carrot sticks

Add bacon to breakfast to increase calories and to prevent hunger on the course.

Sample Meal Plan for Afternoon Exercise

Time	Meal	Food
7:00 a.m.	Breakfast	Turkey patty
		Spinach sautéed in coconut oil
		Blueberries
10:00 a.m.	Snack	Ground turkey lettuce wraps
		Romaine lettuce
		Avocado
		Hot sauce (optional)
1:00 p.m.	Lunch	Herb roasted chicken leg, mixed green salad, carrots, cucumbers, red onion, avocado and olive oil and balsamic vinegar dressing
2:00–3:00 p.m.	Exercise	Water with pinch of unrefined salt and BCAAs
3:30 p.m.	Postworkout Meal #1	Whey protein shake
		Half-cup pineapple juice
		Half-cup frozen strawberries
5:00 p.m.	Postworkout/ Game Meal #2	Steamed jasmine white rice
		Roasted chicken breast
		Sauerkraut
8:00 p.m.	Snack	Roast beef slices and cucumbers

If you're a golfer that needs to lose weight, just have the protein powder post-workout.

If you're a golfer that needs to gain weight, double the juice and strawberries post-workout.

Sample Meal Plan for Afternoon Golf

Time	Meal	Food
7:00 a.m.	Breakfast	Turkey patty Spinach sautéed in coconut oil Blueberries
10:00 a.m.	Snack	Ground turkey lettuce wraps Romaine lettuce Avocado Hot sauce (optional)
12:30 p.m.	Lunch	Herb roasted chicken leg, mixed green salad, carrots, cucumbers, red onion, avocado and olive oil and balsamic vinegar dressing
1:00–5:00 p.m.	Golf	Water with pinch of unrefined sea salt and BCAAs and snacks on the course
5:30 p.m.	Postgolf Meal	Steamed jasmine white rice Roasted chicken breast Sauerkraut
7:30 p.m.	Snack	Roast beef slices and cucumbers

Add extra olive oil or avocado to salad at lunch to increase calories and to prevent hunger on the course.

10 Quick Breakfast Options

For pages and pages, I've been going on about the importance of breakfast, and I've made many arguments for why you can't skip it. If you're in the camp that says you don't have time to make breakfast, I've come up with the following recipes to remove this excuse for you.

Perfect Hardboiled Eggs

The classic hardboiled egg is about the easiest meal to make and grab on the go. Here's how to cook it: Bring a pot of water to a boil and then gently add a few eggs with a slotted spoon. Boil for seven minutes if you want eggs with a custard-like center. Boil for eight minutes if you want more of a molten center. You can boil a dozen eggs on Sunday and have your breakfast protein covered for the whole week in one shot.

Bone Broth & Apple

This is perfect for people who don't have much of an appetite in the morning. Two cups will give you about 20 grams of protein, but you can drink it as easily as coffee. As an added benefit, it contains minerals and electrolytes that will help keep you hydrated throughout a round of golf. Simply heat a two cups' worth in a pan, then add a pinch of unrefined sea salt and pour it into a coffee mug. Add one tablespoon of coconut oil to increase the fat intake and keep you satiated. You can drink this on the way to the course. Then eat an apple to add in fiber for blood sugar stability. Go to *www.bone-broth.com* to purchase broth from chicken or beef.

Gluten-Free (GF) Turkey Power Wrap

Lightly toast a gluten-free (GF) tortilla (Mission makes a great one) and lay four slices of turkey on it. Thinly slice half an avocado on top of the turkey and then add two or three slices of romaine lettuce. Dress with mustard.

Chocolate-Lover's Power Oatmeal

Soak half a cup of GF oatmeal the night before. The soaking helps you digest the oats. In the morning, add a scoop of whey protein to the oats and mix thoroughly. Add a teaspoon of cacao nibs and a small handful of slivered almonds and stir.

Peanut Butter Coconut Breakfast Squares

This is a high protein and fat breakfast bar. Dump 8 ounces of organic, finely shredded coconut into a large mixing bowl. Add half a cup of organic coconut oil, half a cup of chunky organic peanut butter, and four scoops of chocolate protein powder. Wear a pair of food service gloves and mix thoroughly. The coconut oil may be hard, but the heat from your hands will melt it. Evenly spread the mixture onto a 9 x 13 inch cookie sheet and refrigerate for three hours.

Use a large knife and cut the dough into 2 x 2 inch squares. These bars are rich, so you'll only a few until you're satiated. Keep refrigerated, or they'll melt in hot weather.

Meat-Lover's Breakfast: Leftover Meat Sautéed in Butter or Coconut Oil with Spinach

I'm a big fan of leftovers for breakfast. Use whatever meat you have left over from dinner, chopped into small squares. Sauté them in butter or coconut oil along with three handfuls of spinach. Make sure to add unrefined sea salt to taste and pepper too.

Veggie Egg Scramble

Chop up any type of veggie and sauté it in coconut oil over medium heat. Once the veggies are soft, crack in a few eggs. Start to mix the eggs and veggies together until fully cooked.

Apple Cinnamon Pancakes

Traditional pancakes have a ton of refined carbs, but if you make your own you can load them with protein, fat, and fiber. Use GF oats as your base. Place half a cup of GF oats in a blender (Vitamix works the best). Then crack in one whole egg, one scoop of protein powder, and half a teaspoon of cinnamon. Blend the mixture to a creamy texture. Heat a pan with a teaspoon of butter (yes, butter!) and pour the mixture into the center of the pan. Cook for about thirty seconds then flip for another thirty seconds. Add chopped apples on top and enjoy!

The Green Machine Power Smoothie

I know I said not to drink a protein shake for breakfast, but this is a different type of smoothie made up of whole foods. It's liquid, but the addition of PFF from whole foods will slow down the digestion of the drink and keep you full for a while.

Place the following ingredients into a blender:
- 1 cup coconut milk
- 1 handful spinach
- 1 scoop of vanilla protein powder
- 1 tablespoon almond butter
- 1 cup of frozen berries
- 3 drops of stevia for a bit of sweetness
- 1 cup ice (optional)

Breakfast soup

A bowl of soup is nice on a cold day before a round of golf. It's especially good for stabilizing blood sugar. An easy way to make soup in the morning is to purchase a bag of frozen bone broth from *bonebroth.com*. Submerge the bone broth in hot water and let it stand a few minutes.

As the broth defrosts, cut up two carrots and two celery sticks into small pieces. Take any leftover meat you have handy and cut it into cubes. At this point, the broth should be slightly defrosted. Dump the broth into a pot with all the veggies and meat. Once the broth is boiling, simmer five to seven minutes (or until veggies are soft) and serve.

14
ON THE COURSE

Yes, I talked about breakfast before, but I'm going to talk about it again, and again, and again! If you fail to eat breakfast, you simply won't perform optimally on the course. Don't miss this opportunity to create your baseline of blood sugar and establish great energy levels for the entire day. The following are some strategies to help you start mornings off right and make the most of your golf rounds.

Plan to Succeed

You don't want to be stuck on the course with soda and candy bars as your only nutrition options. Plan your day the night before, in the morning, the week before ... whatever it takes. Always have a game plan when it comes to your fuel on the course. Don't underestimate the power of food.

The first priority is to measure your water intake for the round. Remember, you should have 50% of your intake for the day in your golf bag. If you weigh 200 pounds, drink 100 ounces for the day, and half of that amount should be in your bag. This means 50 ounces of water for the round.

For every liter of water, add unrefined sea salt, the natural electrolyte. Just a small pinch should suffice. If you drink the water, and it tastes like the ocean, you put way too much in your water bottle. You do NOT need any sports drink. If you have properly hydrated in the morning and have eaten a good breakfast, you will be fine with water and salt.

Now, start thinking about the food you want to bring with you in your bag. The same principle applies to snacks as well as meals. You want to maintain level blood sugar created with a high-protein breakfast, so your snack foods may not change much from breakfast. Think of your best friend when it comes to blood sugar control: PFF. You still want high-protein foods for the BCAAs and fats for stabilizing blood sugar. You don't need massive amounts carbs for energy during a round. Here is a list of great golf snacks:

- jerky (beef, bison, elk, deer, turkey)
- seeds (sunflower, pumpkin, sesame)
- nuts (almonds, cashews, macadamia, pecans, walnuts)
- celery sticks
- carrot sticks
- natural trail mix with dry fruit (don't get anything with chocolate, candy, or other processed foods in it)
- fruit (always combine with nuts, seeds, or jerky for blood sugar balance)

Protein Bars
There are so many bars on the market, and some are permissible when you don't have access to whole foods.

When choosing a bar, make sure you follow these rules:
- The fewer the ingredients the better
- Choose organic when possible
- Choose one with coconut if possible (again, think fat and fiber)
- It should be gluten-free
- It should be dairy-free

At the same time, avoid these ingredients like the plague (I wouldn't give them to my worst enemy)
- Soy protein products (very processed)
- Partially hydrogenated anything (fake fat)

Sports Drinks

Sports drink companies have us all thinking we need their beverage all the time — even when we aren't playing sports. I have to admit the commercials are very cool, showing athletes sweating blue, green, yellow, or red liquid out of their pores.

But the truth is sports drinks may be necessary for athletes performing continuous exercise for more than one and a half hours at a time. The key word here is continuous. Athletes who compete in triathlons, marathons, cross-country running, or other endurance sports may need to consume some kind of carbohydrate drink for fuel.

Golf is not an endurance event. I remember Dave Phillips, cofounder of the Titleist Performance Institute, saying, "Golf is really not that long to play. The actual physical act of swinging a golf club lasts only two to three minutes — cumulatively — in an entire round!"

The rest of the time you're in a cart. Even if you walk and carry your own clubs, walking a course does not require a tremendous amount of endurance. You walk a few hundred yards at most, then you take your shot, wait for your partner, and walk again at a leisurely pace. Golf is not a form of continuous exercise, so you don't need sugar drinks to fuel your golf game.

Eating Frequency

Once you've established stable blood sugar with breakfast, you want to maintain it throughout the round. Any drop in blood sugar is going to affect you mentally and physically. University of Wales researchers demonstrated that grazing — eating small amounts of food repeatedly over a long period of time — is better for cognitive performance and mood than large doses of food taken in sporadically. This particular study looked at the difference between splitting up calories into two meals versus four meals, and the four-meal approach proved more effective.

What this means for you is eating a huge breakfast and then waiting to eat lunch at the end of the round is a mistake. Your breakfast should be substantial, but then you should have snacks throughout the round. Here are three scenarios for proper snacking during a round.

Option 1

Hole	SNACK
6	Beef jerky with nuts
12	Nuts and apple

Option 2

Hole	SNACK
5	Beef jerky with nuts
10	Nuts and apple
15	Trail mix or beef jerky with nuts

Option 3

Hole	SNACK
4	Beef jerky with nuts
8	Nuts and apple
12	Beef jerky with nuts
16	Nuts

If you currently do not eat any snacks during a round, start with option one. Just starting to eat during a round can be an adjustment, so two snacks is enough to start. Don't think more is better and immediately go to option three. If you eat too much food, it will slow you down on the course.

Play with the three options of snacks above to see what works for you. Some may need four snacks through the round to maintain blood sugar. Others may only need two.

If you are the type of person who forgets to eat, use an alarm to remind you. That way you will never forget to eat a snack. Some of my players on tour have their caddies remind them to eat.

I Forgot!

I often meet players at seminars who say, "What do I eat if I forget my snack?"

If you get to the course and don't have your snack, you're stuck with the club's snack cart or bar. At this point, you must pick the best option in the situation given.

Stabilizing blood sugar is still the priority. The snack cart and halfway house don't have your best interests in mind, so the options will be very spotty. I want to make sure you are well aware of the choices that will make your blood sugar skyrocket so you will at least know which foods to avoid like the plague. Stay away from the following:

- **Alcohol.** Only drink it if you don't care how you play.
- **Bread** (bagels, toast, croissants, anything with wheat). It will make you bloated and actually reduce your ability to use your core muscles during your swing.
- **Candy bars.** You'll feel good for half an hour and then want to take a nap.
- **Chicken tenders.** Anything fried is not good for you, period.
- **French fries.** The USDA says they are a vegetable, but use some common sense.
- **Granola bars.** They sound healthy but are just a glorified candy bar.
- **Juice.** Think liquid sugar. Unlike whole fruit, juice has had the fruit's fiber removed
- **Soda/sports drinks.** Sports drinks have the same sugar as soda. Companies tout the benefits of electrolytes in their drinks. However, the electrolyte amounts are too insignificant to make any difference.

Now that we've gotten the no-nos out of the way, here are the healthier options at your club.

- cup of chicken or tuna salad
- fruit
- hamburger without the bun
- hot dog without the bun
- hard-boiled egg
- nuts
- peanuts
- sunflower seeds

Any combination of these foods will get the job done to stabilize blood sugar while you're on the course.

GEEK MOMENT: YOUR GUT-CORE CONNECTION

Remember the last time you felt really bloated after a meal? I bet you didn't feel like performing any exercise, least of all core exercise. The bloating is a symptom of inflammation in the gut. This inflammation can lead to a viscero-somatic reflex inhibition. Viscero means organ, and somatic means body. Think of a heart attack. The typical reaction is to grab the chest, because the pain from the heart is affecting the chest musculature. In the same way, the gut (viscero) can affect the core muscles (somatic) because they're connected to the same nerves.

University of Barcelona researchers have shown that bloating inhibits (reflex inhibition) the recruitment of muscles such as the rectus abdominis and external oblique and a complete relaxation of the internal oblique. Any physical therapist, chiropractor and fitness professional knows how important these muscles are for rehabilitation and sports performance. Not good if you're trying to maximize the recruitment of core muscles to drive the ball off the tee. Worse yet, the reduced activity of core muscles can set you up for injury in the low back.

Over the many years of food intolerance testing with players, I've concluded the worst culprits causing inflammation are alcohol, wheat, and dairy. If eating these foods cause bloating and gas, then it's critical to avoid them.

15
FAQS ABOUT
USER'S MANUAL

I'm playing in a foursome on a long course, and I expect it will take at least five hours to play. Should I eat any differently based on that?

Golf is a completely different animal when it comes to your eating. Most sporting events will take about half the time. Since your ability to eat during the round will be limited, it's important to eat enough at breakfast.

A long time ago, I was experimenting with fat intake. I fried up one entire package of bacon and left the lard in the pan. I fried five eggs in the lard and sautéed cabbage in the lard as well. I ate all of it — it tasted incredible — and I felt very full. It was an extreme thing to do, but experimentation is very important.

I normally feel hungry three hours after eating. But the extreme amount of fat made me very full. In fact, I didn't want to think about food for more than six hours. I ended up eating my next meal eight hours later. I learned firsthand from this experiment that fat is very satiating and provided a ton of energy.

If you have a long round — or a long day — ahead of you, make sure you eat plenty of protein add fat to your breakfast. For instance, if you normally eat a few eggs and fruit for breakfast, and some fat along with it. Adding a few strips of bacon or an avocado to breakfast will ensure your blood sugar stays stable through the round. Since you'll be satiated, you won't be thinking about food, so you can focus on the next shot. Just make sure you don't eat the whole package of bacon like I did!

How much time should I allow for digestion before a round?

Digestion will vary from person to person. There are no hard and fast rules when it comes to digestion time. You need to experiment with prematch meals.

Back in college, I had a friend who was my roommate and training partner. We would train extremely hard each session. I normally ate about an hour before the gym. But on leg days I would eat my preworkout meal two hours before a leg training session. If you've ever trained legs intensely, sometimes you can lose your lunch — literally.

One time, as I was preparing for a brutal leg day, I walked out to the kitchen, and to my surprise, my roommate was eating a huge plate of food. I asked him, "Aren't you going to train legs today?" He just smiled and said, "Yes!" I responded, "Dude, you're going to puke after eating all that food!" He just smiled and kept eating. I suggested we wait to head to the gym so he could digest, but he insisted we go. We headed to the gym and began the workout. We performed high-rep squats, but to my surprise, my buddy never even got nauseous. I just shook my head. I never would have been able to train immediately after eating the same amount of food.

Some may need an hour to digest before practice or training. Some may need two hours. You'll have to experiment to find what works best for you. But common sense should tell you the more you eat, the more time you'll need to digest.

I skip breakfast because I'm not hungry. What can I do to improve my appetite?

You should gradually build up to a big breakfast. Start by eating something small in the morning. Try a hard-boiled egg with a handful of blueberries. Remind yourself that when you start eating breakfast, you'll be less likely to overeat at night.

I get bored eating the same foods every day. What can I do to stay on track without getting sick of the same foods?

Rotate your foods. For example, eggs are a great source of protein for breakfast, but you shouldn't eat them everyday. Not that eggs are bad for you, but I wouldn't want you to become bored of eating eggs every day. I recommend you eat eggs two to three times per week. You could have eggs one day, chicken sausage another, leftover steak on day three, and then go back to eggs on the fourth day. This is a great way to safeguard against the boredom of foods and to introduce other types of foods into your plan.

I keep hearing about athletes switching to a vegetarian diet. Is it better for my health and performance on the course?

Vegetarian experts love to point to the negative effects of meats. They say meats can be toxic, hard to digest, and cause heart disease. There is some truth to this, depending on the quality of the meat. As mentioned earlier, grain-fed beef is a completely different food than grass-fed beef. If you primarily consume grass-fed beef, you have nothing to worry about.

Vegetarians claim meats are hard to digest and rot in the stomach. This is based on the fact that many people have compromised digestion. Part of the reason is because they don't chew their food efficiently. Another factor is many people do not produce enough hydrochloric acid (HCL) in their stomachs. Acid is associated with burning of the throat and reflux, but that's when it's dysfunctional. HCL is critical for the breakdown of protein in the stomach before it's passed on to the small intestine.

If you're that person who says "meat doesn't agree with me," it's probably due to the fact you don't have enough HCL in your stomach. Simply adding lemon or apple cider vinegar to your meals will do wonders for digestion. Other factors, such as eating quickly on the go, compromise the production of HCL too. It's not the meat that's bad but the lack of chewing and HCL that's the issue.

There's a trend of professional athletes eating a vegetarian diet. These athletes have reported improvements in their health and performance. What you don't know is many of these athletes have a history of eating a lot of junk foods. Professional athletes are "genetic freaks." They're professional athletes in spite of what they eat. As some of these athletes become older, they realize their body doesn't function as well as it used to. They look to change their diets to improve performance. At this point, any positive change such as eating more vegetables as well as the reduction of processed foods makes a difference.

The big difference between a vegetarian diet and an animal-based diet is the protein content. Protein is usually much lower in a vegetarian diet. Over time, many vegetarian athletes will notice that recovery is hampered by the lack of protein. Remember that all ligaments, tendons, connective tissue, and muscle are repaired by protein.

I remember working with a young basketball player who injured his back. He was in so much pain that he couldn't play. I discovered he had a disc bulge at the L5/S1 area of the spine. This is quite rare in young athletes unless there was a severe trauma. He also had a habit of spraining his ankles running down the court. Even when he was exercising properly he would become injured.

After some investigating, he told me he was a vegetarian from birth. His mother thought it would be best. I explained the lack of protein in his diet prevented his connective tissue from repairing. After some convincing, he was willing to try animal protein. He was curious and afraid at the same time. He started with chicken, and to his surprise, he loved it. He couldn't get enough of it. As weeks went by he added fish and eventually red meat.

His injuries began to diminish, and he was pain-free after two months of eating meat. This may be an extreme case, but it shows protein — complete protein from animal sources — is very important for recovery.

When I'm running late, I like to get fast food for breakfast. Do I have any options there?

Every fast-food restaurant has some type of egg sandwich with bacon on the menu. The priority is to get some protein and fat, so eat the eggs and bacon and toss the bread. At least you'll flatline your blood sugar before stepping on the course. This food won't contain organic or high-quality ingredients, but it's the best option in this situation.

16
RECIPES

Cooking your own food is the best way to take maximum control of your nutrition. Even if you're new to cooking, you'll find the meal options simple, but tasty, fast, and easy-to-make staples in your diet.

You're going to notice recipes that use large amounts of food. Some of these could potentially feed a family of eight. This doesn't mean I want you to eat all this food at one sitting. I'm showing you how to cook in bulk. It's especially helpful and cost-effective when it comes to protein sources. Leftover protein sources will be your go-to when you're in a bind. They're also the most time-consuming foods to make, so having them easily accessible will take stress off of you.

I've separated the recipes into a protein section, vegetable section, and starch section. You can mix and match any of the proteins with veggie recipes for breakfast, lunch, or dinner. If you want a frittata for dinner, go for it. If you want Kalua pork with cabbage slaw for breakfast, that's fine too. Combine them as you please, but remember that your BFF for blood sugar control is PFF — protein, fat, and fiber. Make sure to combine a protein with a veggie to create a perfect PFF meal. Use the starches as add-ons to postexercise meals and after finishing a round of golf.

A Word About Seasonings: Herbs and Salt

To make healthy food tasty, you need to master seasonings. Strive to purchase organic fresh and dry herbs just as you do your meats, fruits, and veggies. Remember that not all salt is the same, either. Unrefined sea salt has over eighty trace minerals, while table salt is merely sodium chloride.

Protein

PERFECT SOFT BOILED EGGS

- 6 organic free-range eggs
- unrefined sea salt
- pepper

Bring a small pot of water to a boil. Make sure to use a shallow pot for this so it will be easy to place the eggs into the boiling water. Use a slotted spoon to submerge each egg. If you drop them in, they'll crack, so be gentle! Once you have all six eggs in, boil the eggs for 7 minutes. This will give you a yolk that has a custard-type texture. If you want a more solid yolk, cook for 8 minutes. Once the time is up, transfer the eggs into a cold-water bath to stop the cooking process. You can crack open the eggs while they're warm or wait until they're completely cool. A quick egg-cracking tip is to tap the widest part of the egg then roll the egg, which will break up the rest of the shell. Then peel and enjoy with salt and pepper.

AMAZING CILANTRO CHICKEN

- 1 1/2 lemons
- 1/3 cup olive oil
- 3 cloves garlic
- 1 tablespoon unrefined sea salt
- 2 teaspoons pepper
- 1 bunch cilantro
- 3 lbs organic free-range chicken (boneless, skinless chicken thighs are best)

Add everything but the chicken to a blender and blend for a smooth sauce. Pour the marinade over the chicken and massage it thoroughly to make sure the chicken is fully covered. Marinate the chicken overnight until you are ready to cook. If you don't have that much time, add an additional 1/2 to 1 lemon to encourage quicker marinating. Preheat a grill (or grill pan on your stove) for 2–3 minutes on high until hot and add the chicken. Reduce the heat to medium and cook the chicken, turning twice, for 10–12 minutes total. If you decide to use breast meat, cut the grill time to 8–10 minutes, otherwise you'll have cilantro jerky chicken!

SAVORY PORK ROAST

- 2 teaspoons Celtic Sea Salt
- 2 teaspoons ground pepper
- 2 teaspoons ground cumin
- 2 teaspoons ground coriander
- 2 teaspoons dried oregano
- 1 boneless pork loin (2 1/2 pounds)

Preheat oven to 425°F. Mix the salt, pepper, cumin, coriander, and oregano into a mixture. Rub mixture onto the pork until it's completely covered. Place pork in the center of an oven pan with the fat side up.

Roast until the meat registers 145°F on an instant-read thermometer. Typically this takes 30–40 minutes. Let the meat stand for 10 minutes before cutting into it. Once it's cool, cut it as thinly as possible. The leftovers are great for salads, wraps, or finger foods.

GRASSFED BURGER PATTIES

- 3 lbs grass-fed ground beef
- 3 teaspoons unrefined sea salt
- 3 teaspoons pepper
- 3 teaspoons onion powder

Preheat a grill or pan for 2–3 minutes until hot. Place all the ingredients in a mixing bowl and mix the dry ingredients thoroughly into the meat with your hands. Pick up a fist-size piece of the mixture and roll it into a nice ball. Then smash the ball between your two hands into a burger patty. Reduce the heat to medium and cook the patty 4–5 minutes on each side. If you want a rarer burger, cook 3–4 minutes a side.

TASTY MEATBALLS

- 4 pounds of ground meat
- 2 whole eggs
- 3/4 cup gluten-free bread crumbs
- 1/2 cup diced cilantro
- 1 tablespoon garlic powder
- 1 tablespoon onion powder
- 4 teaspoons unrefined sea salt
- 2 teaspoons pepper

Preheat oven to 375°F. Place all the ingredients in a mixing bowl and mix the dry ingredients thoroughly into the meat. Use a small ice-cream scooper to make balls and place them evenly on a baking sheet. The fat from the meat will prevent sticking, so there's no need to add cooking spray to the baking sheet. Bake for 20 minutes.

CROCKPOT SMOKED KALUA PORK
- 4 pounds bone-in pork shoulder
- 2 tablespoons Hawaiian sea salt
- 1 tablespoon onion powder
- 1 tablespoon garlic powder
- 1 teaspoon pepper
- 1 tablespoon liquid smoke flavoring

Rub all the dry ingredients into the pork and place in the crockpot with the fat side up. Drizzle liquid smoke all over the pork. Place 2 bay leaves on top. Set the machine on low for 8–10 hours. Do not open lid while cooking. The meat will fall off the bone when finished.

FIESTA-STYLE GROUND MEAT
- 2 teaspoons unrefined sea salt
- 2 tablespoons chili powder
- 1 teaspoon garlic powder
- 1 teaspoon onion powder
- 1/2 teaspoon crushed red pepper flakes
- 1/2 teaspoon dried oregano
- 1 teaspoon paprika
- 1 tablespoon ground cumin
- 1 teaspoon pepper
- 2 lbs ground meat (grass-fed if it's beef)

The great thing about this recipe is you can use any ground meat you enjoy. It works well with beef, turkey, chicken, pork, and my favorite: bison! Mix all the dry ingredients in a small bowl. Place a skillet over medium heat and, once hot, place the 2 pounds of meat into it. (Note: You won't need oil unless you choose turkey or chicken breast). Once it begins to brown, start to mix the meat to break it up. Once you've broken up the meat and it's almost fully brown, add in the dry ingredients and mix thoroughly.

FRITTATA FOR DAYS: GF & DF

- 6–8 large free-range organic eggs
- 1/4 cup fresh basil, chopped
- 1 tablespoon olive oil
- 1/2 cup celery, chopped
- 1 small red onion, finely chopped
- 2 cloves minced garlic
- 1 medium zucchini, chopped
- 1 medium yellow squash, chopped
- unrefined sea salt to taste
- pepper to taste

Preheat the oven to 400°F. In a medium bowl, whisk the eggs and basil with a small pinch of salt. Set aside. In an oven-safe, cast-iron skillet, heat olive oil and sauté all the veggies until soft and add salt and pepper to taste. Add the egg mixture to the skillet by pouring it over the veggies. Place the skillet in the center of your preheated oven and bake 13–15 minutes, until it is golden brown.

TENDER JUICY FLANK STEAK

- 3 lbs grass-fed flank steak
- 3 teaspoons garlic powder
- 3 teaspoons onion powder
- 3 teaspoons unrefined sea salt
- 1 1/2 teaspoons pepper
- 3 teaspoons paprika (optional)

Lay out the flank steak on wax paper. Mix all the dry ingredients in a bowl and then coat both sides of the meat with them until fully covered. Refrigerate the steak overnight to maximize flavor. When you're ready to grill, leave the steak out for 20 minutes at room temperature for an even cook. Preheat the grill.

Once the grill is hot, sear each side for 4 minutes and then grill for another 4 minutes on each side for a medium rare steak. Make sure to rest the meat for 10 minutes after grilling before slicing (and slice against the grain).

HEALTHY GRILLED SALMON STEAKS

1–2 pounds wild salmon
1–2 teaspoons unrefined sea salt
1 teaspoon pepper

Salt and pepper is the best and only seasoning you need for wild salmon. Salt and pepper both sides of the fish and place on a hot grill. General rule of thumb is to grill 4–5 minutes each side for a 1-inch thick steak. Be careful to watch the salmon, since the oils may drip down, causing major flare-ups. Adjust the grill as needed.

REFRESHING CILANTRO MAHI-MAHI

- 1 1/2 lemon
- 1/3 cup olive oil
- 3 cloves garlic
- 1 tablespoon unrefined sea salt
- 2 teaspoons pepper
- 1 bunch cilantro
- 3 pounds mahi-mahi

Add all ingredients but the fish to a blender and blend into a smooth sauce. Pour the marinade over the fish and massage it thoroughly to fully cover each piece. Marinate 6–8 hours until you are ready to grill. Preheat the grill for 2–3 minutes until hot. Reduce the heat to medium and add the fish. Cook the fish 3–4 minutes each side.

DUTCH OVEN HERB-ROASTED CHICKEN

- 1/2 cup butter
- 1 cup sage, chopped
- 1 cup thyme, chopped
- 2 tablespoons unrefined sea salt
- 1 tablespoon pepper
- 5 whole garlic cloves, minced
- 1 whole organic chicken
- 2 large onions, chopped

Preheat oven to 450°F. Melt the butter in a pan over the stove and add the chopped herbs, salt, pepper, and garlic. Rub the butter mix under the skin of the chicken and on top. Tie the legs with kitchen twine. Place the chicken in a Dutch oven and bake for 15 minutes. Then turn the oven down to 350°F, bake for another 25 minutes, place the Dutch oven lid on top. Cook until the internal temperature of chicken is 165°F in the thigh. Let the chicken sit for 10 minutes then serve.

Vegetables

FRESH CHOPPED CUCUMBER SALAD

- 3 English cucumbers
  (Persian cucumbers are also great)
- 1 package grape tomatoes
- 1/2 red onion
- 1/2 bundle of Italian parsley
- 2 1/2 lemons (3/4 cup of lemon juice)
- 1/4 cup olive oil
- unrefined sea salt to taste
- Pepper to taste

Dice up all the vegetables and herbs and place them in a container or resealable plastic bag. Squeeze the lemons onto the veggies and then add the olive oil. Let the vegetable marinate in the juices and then add salt and pepper to taste when ready to serve.

CAULIFLOWER MASH

- 1 head cauliflower, broken into chunks
- 1 red onion, diced
- 1–2 cloves garlic, diced
- 3 tablespoons organic coconut oil
- 1 teaspoon unrefined sea salt
- 1/2 teaspoon pepper to taste

Cut up the cauliflower into small florets. Steam the cauliflower until you can poke a fork through it (cook more if you like it the consistency of mashed potatoes). Sauté the onion and garlic in the oil until lightly brown. Drain excess water off the cauliflower and add it to the pan with the onion and garlic. Mash the cauliflower with a potato masher until it is broken down. Add salt and pepper to taste.

CRISPY COOL CABBAGE SLAW
- 1 green cabbage, thinly sliced
- 1/2 purple cabbage, thinly sliced
- 3 carrots, shredded
- 1/2 bunch cilantro, diced
- 1/2 red onion, diced
- 1/3 cup olive oil
- 1/3 cup balsamic vinegar
- 3 tablespoons agave nectar
- 1 teaspoon salt
- 1/2 teaspoon pepper (optional)

Place all ingredients into a large mixing bowl and mix by hand until veggies are thoroughly coated by the liquid ingredients. We eat this at least once or twice a week in our home. My absolute favorite.

RAINBOW SALAD
- 1 head romaine lettuce, sliced into thin strips
- 1/4 purple cabbage
- 1 carrot, grated
- 1/4 bunch cilantro, chopped
- 1/4 red onion, finely diced

Chop all the vegetables and place them in a large mixing bowl. Add the pesto dressing (see page 178) or the creamy Dijon dressing (page 178) and enjoy!

GRILLED ZUCCHINI

- 2 green zucchini
- 2 yellow zucchini
- 1/4 cup olive oil
- unrefined sea salt
- Pepper

This is an easy veggie to cook while you're grilling any meat. Slice zucchini length-wise to about the thickness of your pinky finger. Coat each piece with olive oil and sprinkle on a bit of salt and pepper. Roast on a hot grill for 2–3 minutes each side.

COCONUT STIR-FRY CABBAGE

- 1/2 a green cabbage, thinly sliced
- 1 tablespoon coconut oil
- 1 teaspoon unrefined sea salt
- 1/2 teaspoon pepper

Place a skillet over medium heat and add coconut oil. Add cabbage to pan. Don't panic if it's piled high — the cabbage will shrink. Continue to toss and stir the cabbage until fully cooked. Sprinkle with salt and pepper.

ROASTED BRUSSELS SPROUTS

- 1 bag Brussels sprouts
- 2 tablespoons coconut oil (lard tastes the best)
- 2 tablespoons onion powder
- 1 tablespoon garlic powder
- 1/2 teaspoon unrefined sea salt
- 1/4 teaspoon pepper
- 1/2 cup balsamic vinegar

Preheat oven to 400°F. Chop Brussels sprouts in half and trim the bottoms. Coat the Brussels sprouts with the coconut oil and seasonings. Roast for 20 minutes. Meanwhile, reduce balsamic vinegar by bringing it to a boil then a light simmer under low to medium heat. Occasionally stir until thickened. Toss the Brussels sprouts with the balsamic reduction.

Starch

FRAGRANT STEAMED THAI JASMINE RICE
* 2 cups of Thai jasmine rice
* 1 1/2 cups water

All grains have compounds such as phytic acid that can inhibit the absorption of key minerals. Soaking rice over-night helps to deactivate these compounds. It helps the rice cook faster too. After soaking the rice overnight, dump out the old water and add in one and one half cups of fresh water. Use a rice cooker. This will allow you to use a timer so your rice will be cooked and ready for you when you come home after the gym.

CONVECTION POTATOES
* 4–5 medium-size potatoes

Preheat a convection oven to 425°F. The cooking time for most types of potatoes is similar. You can use russet, Yukon, or sweet potatoes/yams. Rinse the potatoes thoroughly and then poke them several times on each side. Place the potatoes directly on the rack. Cook 40 minutes if you're using longer, thinner potatoes, such as a sweet potatoes or yams. Cook for 50 minutes if cooking rounder potatoes, like russets.

RUSTIC HERB RED POTATOES

- 4 red potatoes, cut into quarters
- 1 tablespoon olive oil
- 1 tablespoon dried rosemary
- 1 teaspoon garlic powder
- 1 teaspoon onion powder
- 1 teaspoon unrefined sea salt
- 1/2 teaspoon pepper

Pre-heat oven to 425°F. Coat potatoes with olive oil and then sprinkle with the dried herbs and other ingredients. Roast for 20 minutes.

COCONUT PLANTAINS

- 1 ripe plantain, peeled and cut into half-inch slices
- 2 teaspoons coconut oil

Place oil in a pan over medium heat and add the plantains. Cook for 2–3 minutes on each side until slightly brown.

COCONUT JASMINE RICE

- 2 cups Thai jasmine rice
- 1 1/2 cups water
- 1 tablespoon coconut oil
- 1 teaspoon unrefined salt

Place rice and water in the rice cooker or pot and add the coconut oil and salt. The oil may be in a clump from sitting at room temperature but will melt once you cook the rice.

Snack

HIGH-PROTEIN COCONUT SQUARES
1 bag organic shredded coconut
(Let's Do Organic brand is the best)
1/2 cup organic coconut oil
1/2 cup crunchy almond butter
3 scoops of PurePaleo (beef) protein powder
4–6 (6 for chocolate lovers!) tablespoons organic cacao nibs

Thoroughly mix all ingredients in a bowl with your hands. Spread the mixture onto a 9 x 13 inch cookie sheet and place in the refrigerator for 2 hours or until the mixture hardens. Use a pizza cutter to cut into squares and enjoy!

Dressings, Sauces & Sides

NO NUTS PESTO DRESSING
- 2 large garlic cloves
- 1/4 cup fresh basil leaves
- 2 teaspoons Lakanto (sugar alternative)
- 1/2 cup olive oil
- 1/2 tsp pepper plus 1/2 tsp salt

Blend all ingredients in a blender until consistency is creamy and smooth. Add it to your salad or even try it as a marinade.

CREAMY DIJON DRESSING
- 3 tablespoons Dijon mustard
- 3 teaspoons salt
- 5 tablespoons apple cider
- 3 tablespoons red wine vinegar
- 1 teaspoon pepper
- 1/4 teaspoon stevia
- 2 cups olive oil

Blend all ingredients except for the olive oil until smooth. Now blend on a low speed and add the olive oil very slowly until the mixture is creamy.

ZESTY GUACAMOLE
- 1 ripe avocado, cut in half with insides scooped out
- 1/2 cup cilantro, chopped
- 1/4 cup red onion, finely diced
- 1/2 lime
- 1/2 teaspoon salt
- 1/4 teaspoon pepper (optional)

Place the avocado flesh in a bowl. Using a fork, mash the avocado until creamy. Add the cilantro, red onion, salt, and pepper. Mix thoroughly, and then squeeze in the lime.

Leftover Meals

MEXICAN BURRITO
- 1 fist worth of green cabbage, thinly sliced
- 1 fist worth of purple cabbage, thinly sliced
- 1–2 decks worth of cooked ground meat

- 1/2 avocado, diced into cubes
- Salsa (optional)

Place the cabbage in a salad bowl. Place the ground meat on top of the cabbage. Add the avocado cubes to the ground meat. If you need a kick, use O'Brother's Organic Habanero Chipotle Hot Sauce or salsa.

POSTWORKOUT MODIFICATION: add in a fist-size portion of jasmine rice or wrap in corn tortillas.

ALL ABOUT PROTEIN BURGER
- 2 teaspoons olive oil
- 1–2 grilled burgers, cut in half
- 4 romaine lettuce leaves
- 1/2 white onion, diced
- Organic mustard to taste
- Organic ketchup to taste
- Pickles (optional)

Add the oil to a medium-hot pan. Throw in the onions and sauté until golden brown. This will bring out the natural sweetness in the onion. Once the onions are finished, heat up the burgers for 2–3 minutes. Place the burgers onto romaine lettuce leaves and top with the onions, mustard, and ketchup. Place another leaf on top of each one and enjoy your burgers.

POSTWORKOUT MODIFICATION: add in a fist-sized portion of jasmine rice or wrap in corn tortillas.

CONCLUSION

I know. That was a lot of info. How ya feelin'?

Overwhelmed? Excited? Those are normal emotions. I bet you have one question: "When will I notice results?"

The answer: It depends. If you feel a bit apprehensive about diving into all these changes head first, start slow. You don't have to incorporate everything all at once. Start at the bottom tier of the pyramid and increase your water intake. Drinking more water alone can make a massive difference.

As a general rule of thumb, give results about three to four weeks to show themselves. As you make changes to your nutrition, there's a metabolic switch that begins immediately. You may feel it and see it in a week. Then again, you may need four weeks. Rest assured, if you're consistent, results are on their way.

Give your body what it needs, and you'll see how many health problems will resolve themselves while performance begins to improve.

If you're interested in more resources on why and how to overhaul your diet, go to *www.robertyang.net* for support. You can find articles and video clips that can help you.

And if you need extra help, shoot me an email and I'll see what I can do for you myself.

Eat well, play well!

REFERENCES

Ahtiainen, J. (2006). Neuromuscular, hormonal and molecular responses to heavy resistance training in strength trained men; with special reference to various resistance exercise protocols, serum hormones and gene expression of androgen receptor and insulin-like growth factor-I. Jyväskylä: University of Jyväskylä, 119.

Andersen, L. L., Tufekovic, G., Zebis, M. K., Crameri, R. M., Verlaan, G., Kjær, M., Suetta, C., Magnusson, P., & Aagaard, P. (2005). The effect of resistance training combined with timed ingestion of protein on muscle fiber size and muscle strength. *Metabolism Clinical and Experimental*, 54, 151–56.

Artifical Turf: Exposures to Ground Up Rubber Tires — Athletic Fields, Playgrounds, Garden Mulch. 2007. Environment of Human Health, Inc. Retrieved from http://www.ehhi.org/reports/turf/turf_report07.pdf.

Bäckhed, F., Ley, R. E., Sonnenburg, J .L., Peterson, D. A., & Gordon, J. I. (2005). Host-bacterial mutualism in the human intestine. *Science*, 307(5717), 1915–20.

Batmanhelidj, F. (1995). *Your body's many cries for water.*

Vienna, VA: Global Health Solutions, Inc.

Belch, J. J .F., Ansell, S., Madhok, R., O'Dowd, A., & Sturrock, R. D. (1988). Effects of altering dietary essential fatty acids on requirements for non-steroidal anti-inflammatory drugs in patients with rheumatoid arthritis: a double blind placebo controlled study. *Annals of the Rheumatic Disease*, 96–104.

Berardi, J. M., Price, T. B., Noreen, E. E., & Lemon, P. W. (2006). Postexercise muscle glycogen recovery enhanced with a carbohydrate-protein supplement. *Med Sci Sports Exerc*, 38(6), 1106–13.

Beynen, A. C. (2004). Fatty acid composition of eggs produced by hens fed diets containing groundnut, soya bean or linseed. NJAS, 52(1), 3–10.

Blomstrand, E., Celsing, F., & Newsholme, E. A. (1988). Changes in plasma concentrations of aromatic and branched-chain amino acids during sustained exercise in man and their possible role in fatigue. *Acta Physiol Scand*, 133(1), 115–21.

Brattström, L., Lindgren, A., Israelsson, B., Andersson, A., & Hultberg, B. (1994). Homocysteine and cysteine: determinants of plasma levels in middle-aged and elderly subjects. *J Intern Med*, 236(6), 633–41.

Brooks, G. A., Fahey, T. D., White, T. P., & Baldwin, K. P. (2000). Exercise physiology: *Human bioenergetics and its applications*. 3. London: Mayfield.

Brown, C. M., Dulloo, A. G., Yepuri, G., & Montani, J. P. (2008). Fructose ingestion acutely elevates blood pressure in healthy young humans. *Am J Physiolo Regul Integr Comp Physiol*, 294(3), R730–7.

Brownstein, D. (2005). *Salt your way to health*. MI: Medical Alternative Press.

Camire, M. E. (1998). Chemical changes during extrusion cooking. Recent advances. *Adv Exp Med Biol*,

434, 109–21.

Carli, G., Bonifazi, M., Lodi, L., Lupo C., Martelli, G., & Viti, A. (1992). Changes in the exercise-induced hormone response to branched chain amino acid administration. *Eur J Appl Physiol Occup Physiol*, 64(3), 272–77.

Candeloro, N., Bertini, I., Melchiorri, G., & De Lorenzo, A. (1995). Effects of prolonged administration of branch-chain amino acids on body composition and physical fitness. *Minerva Endocrinol*, 20(4), 217–23.

Cernak, I., Savic, V., Kotur, J., Prokic, V., Kujic, B., Grbovic, D., & Veliovic, M. (2000). Alternations in magnesium and oxidative status during chonic emotional stress. *Magnes Res*, 13(1), 29–36.

Chek, P. (1999). The golf biomechanic's manual. Encinitas, CA: CHEK Institute.

Cian, C., Koulmann, N., Barraud, P. A., Raphel, C., Jimenez, C., & Melin, B. (2000). Influence of variation of body hydration on cognitive function: effect of hyper hydration, heat stress and exercise-induced dehydration. *J. Psychophysiol*, 14, 29–36.

Clevidence, B. A., Judd, J. T., Schaefer, E. J., Jenner, J. L., Lichenstein, A. H., Muesing, R. A., Wittes, J., & Sunkin, M. E. (1997) Plasma lipoprotein (a) levels in men and women consuming diets enriched in saturated, cis-, or trans-monounsaturated fatty acids. *Arterioscler Thromb Vasc Biol*, 17(9), 1657–61.

Cordain, L., & Friel, J. (2005). *The paleo diet for athletes*. PA: Rodale.

Curi, R., Alvarez, M., Bazotte, R. B., Botion, L. M., Godoy, J. L., & Bracht, A. (1986). Effect of Stevia rebaudiana on glucose tolerance in normal adult humans. *Braz J Med Biol Res*, 19(6), 771–4.

Daley, C. A., Abbott, A., Doyle, P. S., Nader, G. A., &

Larson, S. (2010). A review of fatty acid profiles and antioxidant content in grass-fed and grain-fed beef. *Nutr J.*, 9(10). Published online.

Daly, W., Seegers, C. A., Rubin, D. A., Dobridge, J. D., & Hackney, A. C. (2005). Relationship between stress hormones and testosterone with prolonged endurance exercise. *Euro J Appl Physiol*, 93(4), 375–80.

Darmaun, D., Matthews, D. E., & Bier, D. M. (1988). Physiological hypercortisolemia increases proteolysis, glutamine, and alanine production. *Am J Physiol*, 255(3 Pt1), E366–73.

Dethlefsena, L., & Reimana, D. A. (2011). Incomplete recovery and individualized response of the human distal gut microbiota to repeated antibiotic perturbation. PNAS, 108(1), 4554–4561.

Dhingra, R., Sullivan, L., Jacques, P. F., Wang, T. J., Fox, C. S., Meigs, J. B., D'Agostino, R. B., Gaziano, J. M., & Vasan, R.S. (2007). Soft drink consumption and risk of developing cardiometabolic risk factors and the metabolic syndrome in middle-aged adults in the community. *Circulation*, 116(5), 480–88.

Diamond, T., Wong, Y. K., & Golombick, T. (2013). Effect of oral cholecalciferol 2,000 versus 5,000 IU on serum vitamin D, PTH, bone and muscle strength in patients with vitamin D deficiency. *Osteoporos Int* , 24(3), 1101–5.

Di Pasquale, M. (1997). *Amino acids and proteins for the athlete: The anabolic edge.* Boca Raton, FL: CRC Press.

Enig, M. G. (2000). *Know your fats: The complete primer for understanding the nutrition of fats, oils and cholesterol.* Silverspring, MD: Bethesda Press.

Enig M. G., Atal, S., Keeney M., & Sampugna J. (1990). Isomeric trans fatty acids in the U.S. diet. *J Am Coll Nutr*, 9, 471–86.

Esmarck, B., Andersen, J. L., Olsen S., Richter E. A., Mizuno M., & Klaer M. (2001). Timing of postexercise protein intake is important for muscle hypertrophy with resistance training in elderly humans. *unrefined sea salt* 2001 Aug 15, 535(Pt 1), 301–11.

Fallon, F., & Enig, M. G. (1999) *Nourishing traditions: The cookbook that challenges politically correct nutrition and the diet dictocrats.* Washington, DC: New Trends.

Fife, B. (2004). *The coconut oil miracle.* New York, NY: Penguin Group.

Food and Nutrition Board. Institute of Medicine. (1997). Dietary reference intakes for calcium, phosphorus, magnesium, vitamin D, and fluoride. Washington, DC: National Academy Press.

Fox, M. (1984). *Healthy water for a longer life.* TX: Dunaway Foundation.

Francesconi, R. P., Sawka, M. N., Hubbard, R. W., & Pandolf, K. B. (1989): *Hormonal regulation of fluid and electrolytes:* effects of heat exposure and exercise in the heat. In J. R. Claybaugh & C. E. Wade, Hormonal regulation of fluid and electrolytes (45–85). New York and London: Plenium Press.

Fries, E., Dettenborn, L., & Kirschbaum, C. (2009). The cortisol awakening response (CAR): Facts and future directions. *International Journal of Psychophysiology.* 72(1), 67–73.

Fumeron, F., Brigant, L., Parra, H .J., Bard, J. M., Fruchart, J. C., & Apfelbaum, M. (1991). Lowering of HDL2-cholesterol and lipoprotein A-I particle levels by increasing the ratio of polyunsaturated to saturated fatty acids. *Am J Clin Nutr*, 53, 655–59.

Gill, H. S., & Guarner, F. (2004). Probiotics and human health: a clinical perspective. *Postgrad Med J*, 80,

516–26.

Gleeson, M., & Bishop, N. C. (2000). Modification of immune responses to exercise by carbohydrate, glutamine and anti-oxidant supplements. Immunology and Cell Biology, 78, 554–61.

Greenleaf, J. E., & Sargent, F. (1965). Voluntary dehydration in man. J Appl Physiol, 20, 719–24.

Hakkinen, K., Pakarinen, A., Alen, M., Kauhanen, H., & Komi, P. (1988). Neuromuscular and hormonal adaptations in athletes to strength training in two years. *J Appl Physiol*, 65, 2406–12.

Hathcock, J. N., Shao, A., Vieth, R., & Heaney, R. (2007). Risk assessment for vitamin D. Am J Clin Nutr, 85, 6–18.

Haussinger, D., Roth, E., Lang, F., & Gerok, W. (1993): Cellular hydration state: an important determinant of protein catabolism in health and disease. *Lancet, 341*, 1330–32.

Herrmann, M., Wilkinson, J., Schorr, H., Obeid, R., Georg, T., Urhausen, A., Scharhag, J., Kindermann, W., & Herrmann, W. (2003). Comparison of the influence of volume-oriented training and high-intensity interval training on serum homocysteine and its cofactors in young, healthy swimmers. *Clin Chem Lab Med*, 41(11), 1525–31.

Hewlett, P., Smith, A., & Lucas, E. (2009). Grazing, cognitive performance and mood. *Appetite*, 52(1), 245–8.

Houston, M. (2010). *Prevention & management of vascular aging: the role of nutrition and nutraceuticals in optimizing cardiovascular health!* Biotics Research. Los Angeles, CA.

Howatson, G., Hoad, M., Goodall, S., Tallent, J., Bell, P. G., & French, D. N. (2012). Exercise-induced muscle damage is reduced in resistance-trained males by branched chain amino acids: a randomized, double-blind, placebo controlled study. *J ISSN*, 9, 20.

Ivy, J. L., Katz, A., Cutler, C. L., Sherman, W. M., & Coyle, E. F. (1988). Muscle glycogen synthesis after exercise: effect of time of carbohydrate ingestion. *J Appl Physiol*, *64*(4), 1480–85.

Jovanovic, A., Leverton, E., Solanky, B., Ravikumar, B., Snaar, J. E., Morris, P. G., & Taylor, R. (2009). The second-meal phenomenon is associated with enhanced muscle glycogen storage in humans. *Clin Sci (Lond), Jul 2*, 117(3), 119–27.

Judelson, D. A., Maresh, C. M., Yamamoto, L. M., Farrell, M. J., Armstrong, L. E., Kraemer, W. J., Volek, J. S., Spiering, B. A., Casa, D. J. K., & Anderson, J. A. (2007). Effect of hydration state on strength, power, and resistance exercise performance. *Med Sci sports Exerc*, *39*(10), 1817–24.

Judelson, D. A., Maresh, C. M., Yamamoto, L. M., Farrell, M. J., Armstrong, L. E., Kraemer, W. J., Volek, J. S., Spiering, B. A., Casa, D. J.k, & Anderson, J. A.. (2008). Effect of hydration state on resistance exercise-induced endocrine markers of anabolism, catabolism, and metabolism. *J Appl physiol*; *105*(3), 816–24.

Kabara, J. J. (1984). Antimicrobial agents derived from fatty acids. *Journal of the American Oil Chemists Society*, *61*, 397–403.

Kabara, J. J. (1978). *The pharmacological effects of lipids*. Champaign, IL: The American Oil Chemists Society, 1–14.

Kaplan, R. J., Greenwood, C. E, Winocur, G., & Wolever, T. M. (2001). Dietary protein, carbohydrate, and fat enhance memory performance in the healthy elderly. Am J *Clin Nutr,* 74(5), 687–93.

Khan, H. A., Alhomida, A. S., & Sobki, S. H. (2013). Lipid profile of patients with acute myocardial infarction and its correlation with systemic inflammation. *Biomarck Insight*, 8, 1–7.

Kraemer, W. J. (1988). Endocrine response to resistance exercise. *Med Sci Sports Exerc*, S152–S157.

Lambert, C. P., & Flynn, M. G. (2002). Fatigue during high-intensity intermittent exercise application to bodybuilding. *Sports Med; 32*(8), 511–22.

Lang, T., Streeper, T., Cawthorn, P., Baldwin, K., Taafe, D. R, & Harris, T. B. (2010). Sarcopenia: etiology, clinical consequences, intervention, and assessment. *Osteoporos Int, 21*, 543–59.

Lawrence, G. D. (2013). Dietary fats and health: dietary recommendations in the context of scientific evidence. *Adv. Nutr. 4*, 294–302.

Lenter, C. (1981). Geigy Scientific Tables. 8th edition. Basle: Ciba-Geigy.

Levenhagen, D. K., Gresham, J. D., Carlson, M. G, Maron, D. J., Borel, M.J., & Flakoll, P. J. (2001). Postexercise nutrient intake timing in humans is critical to recovery of leg glucose and protein homeostasis. *Am J Physiol Endocrinol Metab., 280*, E982–E993.

Lord, R. S., & Bralley, J. A. (2008). *Laboratory evaulations for integrative and functional medicine*, 2nd Edition. Duluth, GA: Metametrix Institute.

Madden, J. A. J., Plummer, S. F., Tang, J., Garaiova, I., Plummer, N. T., Herbison, M., Hunter, J. O., Shimada, T., Cheng, L., & Shirakawa, T. (2005). Effect of probiotics on preventing disruption of the intestinal microflora following antibiotic therapy: A double-blind, placebo-controlled pilot study. *Inter Immuno, 5*, 1091–97.

Matzen, L. E., Andersen, B. B., Jensen, B. G., Gjessing, H. J., Sindrup, S. H., & Kvetny, J. (1990). Different short-term effect of protein and carbohydrate intake on TSH, growth hormone(GH), insulin, C-peptide, and glucagon in humans. *ScandJ Clin Lab Invest, 50*(7), 801–5.

McGowan et al. (2013). A proof of principle clinical trial to determine whether conjugated linoleic acid modulates the lipogenic pathway in human breast cancer tissue. *Breast Cancer Res Treat, 138*(1), 175–83.

Newsholme, E. A. (1994). Biochemical mechanisms to explain immunosuppression in well-trained and overtrained athletes. *Int J Sports Med, 15*(3), S142–7.

Newsholme, E. A., Blomstrand, E., Ekblom, B. (1992). Physical and mental fatigue: Metabolic mechanisms and importance of plasma amino acids. *Br Med Bull, 48*(3), 477–95.

Nuernberg, K., Dannenberger, D., Nuernberg, G., Endera, K., Voigta, J., Scollanb, N. D., Wood, J.D., Nutec, G. R., & Richardson, R. I. (2005). Effect of a grass-based and a concentrate feeding system on meat quality characteristics and fatty acid composition of longissimus muscle in different cattle breeds. *Livest Prod Sci, 94*, 137–7.

Oliver, J. M., Affleck, J., Patel, N., Kellett, G. L. (2007). Sweet taste receptors in rat small intestine stimulate glucose absorption through apical GLUT2. *J Physiol 582.1*, 379–2.

Paddon-Jones, D., Westman, E., Mattes, R. D., Wolfe, R. R., Astrup, A., & Westerterp-Plantenga, M. (2008). Protein, weight management, and satiety. *Am J Clin Nutr, 87*(5), 1558S–1561S.

Paik, I. Y., Jeong, M. H., Jin, H. E., Kim, Y. I., Suh, A. R., Cho, S. Y., Roh, H. T., Jin, C. H., Suh, S. H. (2009) Fluid replacement following dehydration reduces oxidative stress during recovery. *Biochem Biophys Res Commun, 383*(1), 103-7.

Pfohl, M., Schreiber, I., Liebich, H. M., Haring, H.U., & Hoffmeister, H.M. (1999) Upregulation of cholesterol synthesis after acute myocardial infarction—is cholesterol a positive acute phase reactant? *Atherosclerosis 142*, 389-93.

Ravaglia, G., Forti, P., Maioli, F., Boschi, F., Cicognani, A., Bernardi, M., Pratelli, L., Pizzoferrato, A., Porcu, S., & Gasbarrini, G. (1997). Determinants of functional status in healthy Italian nonagenarians and centenarians: a comprehensive functional assessment by the instruments of geriatric practice. *J Am Geriatr Soc, 45*(10), 1196-202.

Ringsdorf, W., Cheraskin, E., & Ramsey, E. (1976). Sucrose neutrophilic phagocytosis and resistance to disease. *Dental Survey 52*, No. 12, 46-48.

Roberts, H. J. (1998). Reactions attributed to aspartame-containing products: 551 cases. *Jour Appl Nutr, 40*, 85-94.

Rogers, S. A. (2002) *Detoxify or die*. Sarasota, FL: Sand Key Company.

Ross, J. (1999). *The diet cure*. NY: Penguin Books.

Sadeghi, S., Wallace, F. A., & Calder, P. C. (1999). Dietary lipids modify the cytokine response to bacterial lipopolysaccharide in mice. *Immun, 96*(3), 404-10.

Schoffstall, J. E., Branch, J. D., Leutholtz, B. C., & Swain, D. E. (2001). Effects of dehydration and rehydration on the one-repetition maximum bench press of weight-trained males. *J Strength Cond Res,*

15(1), 102–8.

Sharp, M. H., Lowery, R. P., Shields, K. A., Lane, J. R., Gray, J. L., Partl, J. M., Hayes, D. W., Wilson, G. J., Hollmer, C. A., Minivich, J. R., & Wilson, J. M. (2017). The Effects of Beef, Chicken, or Whey Protein Post-Workout on Body Composition and Muscle Performance. J Strength Cond Res. doi:10.1519/JSC.0000000000001936. [Epub ahead of print]

Shimomura, Y., Inaguma, A., Watanabe, S., Yamamoto, Y., Muramatsu, Y., Bajotto, G., Sato, J., Shimomura, N., Kobayashi, H., & Mawatari, K. (2010). Branched-chain amino acid supplementation before squat exercise and delayed-onset muscle soreness. Int J Sport Nutr Exerc Metab. 20(3), 236–44.

Simopoulos, A. P., Salem, N. Jr. (1989). n–3 Fatty acids in eggs from range-fed Greek chickens. N Engl J Med, 321, 1412.

Simopoulos, A. P. (1991). Omega-3 fatty acids in health and disease and in growth and development. Am J Clin Nutr, 54, 438–63.

Simopoulos, A. P. (1999). The omega diet. New York, NY: Harper Collins.

Spiller, G. A. (2001). Handbook of dietary fiber in human nutrition. Boca Raton, FL: CRC Press.

Stitt, P. (1980). Fighting the food giants. WI: Natural Press.

St-Onge, M. P., & Bosarge, A. (2008). Weight-loss diet that includes consumption of medium-chain triacylglycerol oil leads to a greater rate of weight and fat mass loss than does olive oil. Am J Clin Nutr, 87(3), 621–6.

St-Onge, M. P., & Bosarge, A., T-Goree, L. L., & Darnell, B. (2008). Medium chain triglyceride oil consumption as part of a weight loss diet does not lead to an adverse metabolic profile when compared to olive oil. *J Am Coll Nutr, 27*(5), 547–52.

Szabo, G., Bala, S., Petrasek, J., & Gattu, A. (2011). Gut-liver axis and sensing microbes. *Dig Dis, 28*(6), 737–44.

Thom, E., Wadstein, J., & Gudmundsen O. (2001). Conjugated linoleic acid reduces body fat in healthy exercising humans. *J Int Med Res, 29*(5), 392–6.

Toxic fairways: Risking groundwater contamination from pesticides on long golf courses (1995, December). Attorney General of New York; New York State; Office of the Attorney General Environmental Protection Bureau. Retrieved from http://www.beyondpesticides.org/documents/toxic-fairways-1995.pdf

Tremolaterra, F., Villoria, A., Azpiroz, F., Serra, J., Aguadé, S., & Malagelada, J. R. (2006). Impaired viscerosomatic reflexes and abdominal-wall dystony associated with bloating. *Gastro. 130*, 1062–68.

Ulett, G. A. (1980). Food allergy-cytotoxic testing and the central nervous system. *Psychiatric J Univ Ottawa, 5*, 2100–108.

Van Baak, M. A. (2008). Meal-induced activation of the sympathetic nervous system and its cardio-vascular and thermogenic effects in man. *Physical Behav, 94*(2), 178–86.

Van Loon, L. J., Saris, W. H., Kruijshoop, M., & Wagenmakers, A. J. (2000). Maximizing postexercise muscle glycogen synthesis: carbohydrate supplementation and the application of amino acid or protein hydrolysate mixtures. *Am J Clin Nutr , 72*(1), 106–11.

Voon, P. T., Ng, T. K., Lee, V. K., & Nesaretnam K.

(2011). Diets high in palmitic acid (16:0), lauric and myristic acids (12:0 + 14:0), or oleic acid (18:1) do not alter postprandial or fasting plasma homocysteine and inflammatory markers in healthy Malaysian adults. *Am J Clin Nutr, 94*(6), 1451–7.

Walsh, N. P., Blannin, A. K., Robson, P. J, & Gleeson, M. (1998). Glutamine, exercise and immune function. *Sports Med, 26*(3), 177–191.

Williams, M., Young, J. B., Rosa, R. M., Gunn, S., Epstein, F. H., & Landsberg, L. (1986). Effect of protein ingestion on urinary dopamine excretion. Evidence for the functional importance of renal decarboxylation of circulating 3,4-dihdroxyphenylalanine in man. *J Clin Invest, 78*(6), 1687–93.

Wissem, M., Hassine, A. I. H., Bouaziz, A., Bartegi, A., Thomas, O., & Roig, B. (2011). Effect of endocrine disruptor pesticides: A review. *International Journal of Environmental Research and Public Health. 8*(6), 2265–2303.

Worthington, V. (2001). Nutritional quality of organic versus conventional fruits, vegetables and grains. *J Alt Comp Med., 7*(2), 161–73.

Wright, J. &, Lenard, L. (2001). *Why stomach acid is good for you.* Littlefield Publishing Group: Lanham, M.D.

Zawadzki, K. M., Yaspelkis III, B. B., & Ivy, J. L. (1992). Carbohydrate-protein complex increases the rate of muscle glycogen storage after exercise. J. Appl. Physio, 72, 1854–59.

Zelig, M. (1998). Diet and estrogen status: the cruciferous connection. *J Med Food, 1*(2), 67–81.

INDEX